Consciousness

What You Should Know About It

Joseph Zorskie

ISBN: 1-4392-5144-4
ISBN-13: 9781439251447
Library of Congress Control Number: 2009907529

To order additional copies, please contact us.
BookSurge
www.booksurge.com
1-866-308-6235
orders@booksurge.com

Acknowledgments

Years ago, conversations with a friend in graduate school; Bob Fanelli ignited my interest in matters of the mind. This interest later led to conversations with David Bohm on the same subject.

Scott Forbes was the major force pushing me over the hump of inertia when writing this book seemed very difficult. Together we forged an outline which got me started. Many enjoyable evenings we spent talking about consciousness.

Later, John Hidley was an important sounding board for me. We attended meeting of ASSC together and brainstormed new ideas. Beth Stephans much improved the manuscript with her thoughtful criticisms.

Javier Gomez alerted me to the effects of flashing colors on children. Elizabeth Spring, Harry Spring, Terry Royce, and Patrick Russell read early forms of the manuscript and encouraged me to publish. Elizabeth published her own book and helped in my publishing process. Each of these friends provided helpful suggestions and corrections to my writing.

Major editorial credit goes to Chloe Gladstone, who spent many hours correcting my use of the English language and punctuation. Donn Gladstone created the website, museumofconsciousness.com, which gives access to an early form of the book. Donn also got my image files ready for printing.

Thanks too, to my wife Sharon, who tolerated my research and hours typing and made it easier to finish this project. She also guided me in the design and final version of the cover.

chapter

ONE

"Nosce te ipsum"[1] or "know thyself," is inscribed in stone at the entrance to the Temple of Apollo at Delphi. For Socrates, "The unexamined life is not worth living."[2] Plato likens the common person to one spending life chained in a dark cave. It seems that some people, living two or three thousand years ago, had discovered something. They had opened the door to something they regarded as having the highest value some insight that makes life worth living. What is it they came to know?

That is the sole subject of this book. What they knew, and, more importantly, how we can come to know what is so enriching. Some insight to start the examined life, some insight that makes life worth living...that allows us to peer out of the dark cave.

This is not some secret knowledge passed down through the ages. It appears in the writing of many people who value the examined life. Having read many treatments of this insight, I feel that it deserves more than the sentences or paragraphs that usually suffice to point to it. This topic is not touched on in high school or university, unless one is in a philosophy class. I have never seen it broadcast on television, nor explored in any movie. Yet I feel it is important, and I feel strongly that an entire book is needed to help absorb this key topic... the key to the door of perception.

In what follows, Plato, author of *The Republic,* is relating a conversation between Socrates, Plato's teacher, and another student, Glaucon. We are asked to imagine a person living his whole life in a dark cave. The person is chained to a post in the middle of the cave, in such a manner that he cannot turn his head to see himself or to look out the cave entrance. He faces the rear of the cave. Outside the cave, a small fire perpetually burns and illuminates the back wall of the otherwise dark cave. People and animals often walk past the cave opening and cast their shadows on the back wall. They talk or make sounds, which echo off the back wall. The chained person views the moving shadows and hears the echoes, and this is all he has ever seen or heard. This is his life. He has come to accept the shadow images as the real world.

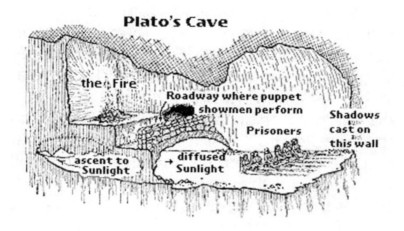

Plato's Cave

We can imagine the shadows pausing and interacting, talking or shouting, perhaps dancing or fighting. But, this shadow world, lacking color and depth, is the entire experience of the chained one. He knows nothing of the world outside his cave; he is not even aware that it exists. He does not know he is in a cave. He does not lament his condition. He is blissful in his ignorance.

Plato's classic "Allegory of the Cave" is a must-read. On the internet you can find thousands of sites that offer translations. Here is a short version, which will serve our purpose.[3]

Socrates is talking to a young follower of his named Glaucon, telling him a fable to illustrate what it's like to be a philosopher—a lover of wisdom:

Socrates: Most people, including ourselves, live in a world of relative ignorance. We are even comfortable with that ignorance, because it is all we know. When we first start facing truth, the process may be frightening, and many people run back to their old lives. But if you continue to seek truth, you will eventually be able to handle it better. In fact, you want more! It's true that many people around you now may think you are weird or even a danger to society, but you don't care. Once you've tasted the truth, you won't ever want to go back to being ignorant!

And now, let me show in a figure how far our nature is enlightened or unenlightened: Behold! Human beings living in an underground den, which has a mouth open toward the light and reaching all along the den;

here they have been from their childhood, and have their legs and necks
chained so that they cannot move,
and can only see before them, being
prevented by the chains from turning
round their heads. Above and behind
them a fire is blazing at a distance,
and between the fire and the prisoners there is a raised way; and you will
see, if you look, a low wall built along
the way, like the screen which mari-
onette players have in front of them,
over which they show the puppets.

Glaucon: I see.

Socrates: And do you see, I said, men
passing along the wall carrying all
sorts of vessels, and statues and figures of animals made of wood and
stone and various materials, which
appear over the wall? Some of them
are talking, others silent.

Glaucon: You have shown me a
strange image, and they are strange
prisoners.

Socrates: Like ourselves; and they see only their own shadows, or the shadows of one another, which the fire throws on the opposite wall of the cave?

Glaucon: True, how could they see anything but the shadows if they were never allowed to move their heads?

Socrates: And of the objects which are being carried in like manner they would only see the shadows?

Glaucon: Yes.

Socrates: And if they were able to converse with one another, would they not suppose that they were naming what was actually before them?

Glaucon: Very true.

Socrates: And suppose further that the prison had an echo which came from the other side, would they not be sure to fancy when one of the passers-by spoke that the voice which they heard came from the passing shadow?

Glaucon: No question.

Socrates: To them, the truth would be literally nothing but the shadows of the images.

Glaucon: That is certain.

Socrates: And now look again, and see what will naturally follow if the prisoners are released and disabused of their error. At first, when any of them is liberated and compelled suddenly to stand up and turn his neck round and walk and look toward the light, he will suffer sharp pains; the glare will distress him, and he will be unable to see the realities of which in his former state he had seen the shadows; and then conceive some one saying to him, that what he saw before was an illusion, but that now, when he is approaching nearer to being and his eye is turned toward more real existence, he has a clearer vision—what will be his reply? And you may further imagine that his instructor is pointing to the objects as they pass and requiring him to name them—will he not be perplexed? Will he not fancy that the shadows which he formerly saw are truer than the objects which are now shown to him?

Glaucon: Far truer.

Socrates: And if he is compelled to look straight at the light, will he not have a pain in his eyes which will make him turn away and take in the objects of vision which he can see, and which he will conceive to be in reality clearer than the things which are now being shown to him?

Glaucon: True.

Plato then asks us to imagine what would happen if our caveman were freed from his bonds and could turn his head and look out the opening of the cave. Imagine his shock at seeing the fire and the people passing, in full light, not in the shadows. Plato writes of the man being blinded by the vision, unable to take it all in. He cannot make sense of it. The shock is overwhelming to him.

I think I am not alone in interpreting this shock as arising not from the painful glare of direct light on eyes accustomed to dim shadows but the shock of seeing that what was taken to be reality (the shadows) was merely an image (a shadow) of reality. The man's world is shaken. His belief in the reality of the shadow show on the back wall of the cave is shaken.

Socrates and Plato are speaking to us with this parable of the cave. They feel we are the ones chained in a cave and accepting the shadows, for a reality beyond our perceptions. The key to unlocking the chains, to releasing ourselves and turning around, so to speak—to see the situation we are in—is to understand the meaning of the parable.

Plato used the fire-cave analogy because in his time, 400 B.C., it was the best available. A more up-to-date version of the tale would be to imagine a person in a windowless room chained to a seat in front of a huge television screen. The images on the screen are created by a video camera outside the room, connected via cable to the room's TV screen. The camera also has microphones to pick up the sounds, which enhance the presentation.

(Color TV)

Like the person in the cave, the person in the room can see animals and people as they pass by the camera, although now, grass, trees, clouds, mountains, etc. are part of the show. Again the person has always been in this room, constrained to view only the screen. The images are in color now, rather than black-and-white shadows, and the sound is far better than the echoes of the cave. Compared to the cave analogy, it is easier to imagine that a person constrained in such a manner could accept these TV images for reality. The screen is huge, and this is all he has ever seen. For such a person, the TV tree is believed to be the real tree, never having seen the tree that is the source of the TV image. The video world is his reality, and more importantly, he does not realize that he is confined to a room. He is unaware of his situation. His reality is in front of him. He knows nothing of real trees, cameras, or TVs.

An even more current version of the parable would be to reduce the cave to the size of a helmet worn by our unsuspecting subject. It could be one of those virtual reality helmets that present to each eye a slightly different image (stereoscopic) on a small but sharp TV screen. The left eye sees an image from a compact video camera mounted on the left side of the helmet, while the right eye sees a different image from a camera fixed to the right side of the helmet. Such an arrangement gives the wearer a stereo view of the world outside the helmet, a three-dimensional representation. When the wearer's head turns, of course, the cameras turn with it, and the images on the TV screens change. The 3-D view now depicts the new direction. This arrangement would allow the wearer to move about and navigate among the objects of the real world while watching the representation of that world from within the helmet. Wearing this device you could change the color of the walls or the pattern on the carpet.

Similar helmets are used in treating people with phobias. For example people with acrophobia, fear of high places, are presented with computer-generated views imitating what would be seen from a tall building. The users report a strong sense of actually being in the virtual reality presented to them, even though the renderings are rather simple. Repeated exposure to these fear-inducing situations can gradually wean a person off the fear.

The military has developed an even more advanced version to train soldiers for dangerous combat situations. The soldier dons a 3-D helmet and enters a large sphere (about 10 feet in diameter). A computer simulates a virtual reality, but now the soldier can walk about in this world. As he walks, his feet turn the sphere, which, via the computer, changes his virtual world appropriately. The soldier gets the sense of walking about in a world...a virtual world created by the computer.

The use of the virtual reality (VR) helmet gives people a strong feeling of being, not in the real world but in the virtual world. If they had worn the device for their entire lives, what we call the virtual world would be their real world. They would be totally deceived.

We can take these thought experiments one step further into science fiction. Michael Lockwood, on page 300 of *Mind, Brain & the Quantum*, asks us to imagine a suit created to help a disabled person.

> Such a person might be suffering from an extreme form of immune deficiency which would make any direct contact with the outside atmosphere fatal. So she's been kitted out, from birth, with a protective suit, rather like a space suit. There are no windows in the suit: it is both light proof and

soundproof. Everything is done by remote sensing. What the person actually sees, sees directly, is a television image, relayed from a pair of video cameras mounted outside the suit, and viewed through stereoscopic lenses. What she actually hears comes from a pair of loudspeakers, wired up to external microphones. And her tactile sensations, rather than being the consequence of forces transmitted directly through the suit, are immediately caused by external sensors. Since this is science fiction, we could imagine all of this being done so cunningly that it was several years before the person herself became aware that she was in any way abnormal: for example, the outside of the suit might be cleverly contrived to look exactly like normal skin (and be able to expand to match the growth of the body it enclosed).

The visionary Ray Kurzweil[4] offers an even more fantastic version of a virtual reality scenario. His claim is that advancements in technology will allow us, in 25 years, to create tiny robots—nanobots— which could be injected into our bodies.

Nanobot technology will provide fully immersive, totally convincing virtual reality. Nanobots will take up positions in close physical proximity to every interneuronal connection coming from our senses...If we want to experience reality, the nanobots just stay in position (in the capillaries) and do nothing. If we want to enter virtual reality, they suppress all of the inputs coming from our actual senses and replace them with the signals that would be appropriate for the virtual environment. Your brain experiences these signals as if they came from your physical body. After all, the brain does not experience the body directly...your brain will experience the synthetic signals just as it would the real ones. You could decide to cause your muscles and limbs to move as you normally would, but the nanobots would intercept these interneuronal signals, suppress your real limbs from moving, and instead cause your virtual limbs to move, appropriately adjusting your vestibular system and providing the appropriate movement and reorientation in the virtual environment.

Finally we come to the last situation to appreciate. Consider your own skull as a protective cave encasing a prisoner—your brain. The brain is constrained to have access only to the input provided by nerve channels. The optic nerves from the eyes pass signals from the retina stimulated by light entering the eye. These nerves conduct a chemical signal (rather slowly) to the brain, which somehow constructs a representation related to the input. This phenomenon, of the brain's own construction, is what the brain (the prisoner) knows. People and animals moving about outside the eye-skull are not directly seen, but sensed via the signals received by the brain.

The ears detect a limited range of vibrations in the air and send nerve signals to auditory parts of the brain, which contribute a sense of sound to the scene. Similar chemical signaling from the nose, tongue, and skin going to different brain areas contribute the sensations of odor, taste, and touch.

Now here's the point: What we see before us is not the real world outside, but a virtual world inside our brain! We all live in a virtual reality. Here, of course, I am using the term "virtual reality" in the modern sense of the worlds computers create with video games. It is our brain that computes and internally displays its best guess as to what is going on outside itself. The internal display includes a representation of our body at the center of the virtual world. Wherever we go, here ever we are—in the middle of it all. We have lived with this scheme since the day we were born and are accustomed to it. Our culture, as it is presently structured, reinforces the notion that our internal display is the real thing. At present, only a very small percentage of people is aware of this fact of perception—that what you see is really you.

This is analogous to the beliefs that existed on our planet up until the 1600s. People believed the Earth to be the center of the universe, with the Sun and other planets revolving around it. For them, the Sun rose in the east, passed overhead, and disappeared in the west. How difficult it must have been for them to accept the notion that the Earth rotates and the Sun does not move around the Earth. Even more difficult would be to accept that the Earth revolves around the Sun and that the Sun is enormously bigger than the Earth. It required a revolution in thought to embrace these facts. A revolution based on careful attention to clues that the geocentric view was wrong. As Copernicus wrote:

> Finally we shall place the Sun himself at the center of the Universe. All this is suggested by the systematic procession of events and the harmony of the whole Universe, if only we face the facts, as they say, "with both eyes open."[5]

Once again you are asked to open your eyes...to the fact that you live in a virtual world. A world of shapes, colors, sounds, odors, and sensations all created in your brain to assist in your survival.

This virtual world is highly detailed, but not as detailed as we might think. Only the very center of our field of vision has enough detail to allow us to read. Focus on any word on this page and try to read a word two or three lines above or below it, and you will get a sense of how quickly the detail fades. We have to shift our vision along each line in order to read it all. The surrounding visual area seems detailed, but it is not.

Our virtual world contains color, sound, smell, taste, and touch (cold, hot, windy, humid, etc.). All these things are laid out in a virtual space, our 3-D world. This phenomenal world, which we experience from birth, supported by our interactions with things and parents and culture, gives us the strong feeling that this phenomenal world is the real world. We do not recognize our part, the brain's part, in all this. We get the incorrect notion that the phenomenon is real, outside of us, and complete, and that we reside in it. In later sections we will explore things that can be shown to exist in the real world but that we cannot sense. Additional "colors," "sounds," etc. that some creatures sense but that we are not privileged to sense except through our instruments. Our virtual world is not complete.

Color, sound, taste, touch, and smell are the qualities of our phenomenal world. The word "quality" derives from a dialogue attributed to Socrates, in which he referred to the "what is-ness" ("po io tes" in Greek) of our experience.[6] The term "common sense" was coined by Aristotle to talk about the place where all the senses come together. We can appreciate that people have been aware of this trick of the mind for a very long time.

For you now, the virtual world may be a book in front of you being held by hands on arms extending from your torso. It looks real, but it is not the real world you are now seeing and feeling. It is your brain's best attempt at depicting the real world around you. The representation is obviously quite good, because it has helped you survive many dangers (crossing streets, climbing trees, avoiding rotten meat). People with inferior representations do not survive. There is survival value in having a superior way of viewing the world.

In computer graphics there is an acronym WYSIWYG (pronounced whiz-e-wig) for "what you see is what you get." When viewing a document or image on your monitor, you are sometimes presented with a display that is a disappointing match with the printed document...particularly if you have selected an unusual font. But some programs can render a good preview of the final print job, a WYSIWYG view. Similarly, we can refer to our internal display of what our senses can grasp of the external world as WYSIRY (pronounced whiz-ery) for "what you see is really you." The acronym is reminiscent of wizardry and mystery, which is vaguely fitting. Another phrase, "The observer is the observed,"[7] is perhaps referring to the same insight, although reversing it. "The observed is the observer" would be more to the mark.

The final analogy, of the brain in the skull, differs from the others in one very important way. The others—the cave, the TV room, the helmet, and the suit—are alike in that they all have an observer looking at a screen. In the brain there is no little observer viewing some brain-screen. Brain research has recently (say in the last 15 years) become very popular, with the number of publications growing exponentially. The functions of the various areas of the brain have been more or less determined. But no area has been found that could function as a screening room, where all the sensory input comes together. This current lack of understanding does not detract from the point of this book. It is the brain—not the heart, liver, kidney, or any other organ—that is necessary for consciousness. Nobody knows just how the brain creates this magic, but centuries of data point to the brain as the central organ of consciousness. Sensory data enter the brain, and…in the brain, conscious experience occurs.

Some philosophers[8] refer to this internal display as the "phenomenal representation." Outside of us are the landscape, trees, people, etc., and inside is what our senses make of it...our brainscape. Plato's prisoner in the cave is a venerable analogy for our situation relative to the world outside our bodies. The shadows and echoes in the cave create the feeling of reality. Similarly, we are imprisoned in our brains, and accept the brain's display—the brainscape—as the primary reality.

Escaping from the Cave

Could the cave-dweller observe the shadow show very closely and gather clues pointing to the fact that they are secondary? Could the chained one figure out that the shadows, although they are real shadows, are not the total reality?

For example: The edges of the shadows are not uniformly sharp. A dog-shaped shadow might be initially large and indistinct but continuously change to be smaller and sharper (as the dog moves from close to the light source toward the cave wall). You can easily recreate this shadow effect by holding your hand near a lamp and casting a large shadow on a wall, then moving your hand toward the wall and observing how the shadow changes from big and fuzzy to hand-sized and sharp.

Another clue: A dog's shadow, its projected image, could be seen to change from having a head, body, four legs, and a tail to having just a body and two legs (as the dog rotates from side view to front view).

Another clue: A person might be seen talking with silhouette lips moving, but then the head turns and the sound continues but the lips are not seen.

Another clue: Shadows moving toward each other can pass through each other, although often one shadow slightly enlarges and the other slightly shrinks (as the movers shift paths to avoid each other).

Taken together, these clues might lead one to conceive of a third dimension, rather than just the two-dimensional world of the shadows. There are many other clues that could be collected, but our goal is not to save the hypothetical prisoner but to gather clues to save ourselves from making the analogous mistake. The prisoner in the cave is offered as an analogy for our situation of the brain in the skull. Any analogy breaks down if it is pushed too far, beyond the limits of its applicability, so we will move on. We should now ask what clues we can gather from our situation that could reveal to us (or convince us of) the mistake we make in accepting appearance as reality.

Dreams and Hallucinations

"Consciousness is that which goes away in dreamless sleep and returns when one awakes."
—Giulio Tononi

"By consciousness I simply mean those subjective states of awareness or sentience that begin when one wakes in the morning and continue...until one falls into a dreamless sleep."
—John Searle

Even in dreamless sleep the brain is very active. Why some brain activity is associated with consciousness and other brain activity is not, is under investigation. Pinning down those brain areas necessary for conscious activity is an important step in uncovering how the brain produces consciousness. The cerebellum at the back of the head is packed with neurons but has no apparent connection with consciousness. Discovering the regions of the brain that are necessary for conscious experience is a subject of ongoing research. But each of us has the opportunity to do some personal research. I am speaking of dreams.

Ordinary dreams are a clue to WYSIRY (what you see is really you), because in dreaming the brain generates a visual/auditory display that can seem very real without input from external sources. Sometimes the dream can include external stimuli. The alarm clock might enter a dream as a fire engine or school bell. I recently had a dream, perhaps motivated by writing this section, in which I picked up a piece of plaid fabric and noticed first the pattern, and then the woven fibers and lastly the tiny hairs on the fibers...highly detailed, that is. Dreams can be so real that children can fear going to sleep.

The regions of the brain that produce these vivid dreams are thought to be the same regions that produce our internal representation of the external world. This is a great clue. Probably you have had the experience of a dream so vivid, so real, that upon awakening you were a bit confused as to dreaming versus waking. This demonstrates to us that our brain is quite capable of generating experiences that can fool us. Knowing that it is possible for the brain to generate a convincing internal display (a vivid dream) without any input from the outside should make it easier to accept the notion that the brain is generating the experience we call consciousness. Consciousness is a sort of waking dream, grounded in information collected by our senses. WYSIRY.

I am not referring to the meaning of dreams, which is a highly debatable topic, nor to the physiological function of dreams (also still a subject of inquiry), but to the brain's obvious capacity to create these internal images. Dreams point out the remarkable capability of the brain to generate convincing images. We make these images in dreams and we make these images in waking life as well. In dreams the source is internal (largely from memory), while in waking life the source is outside us.

Sometimes people report having a dream in which they feel that they have awakened from dreaming. In such dreams the dream environment may be very much like the dreamer's actual home. He may dream of dressing and preparing to go to work...all while still asleep. In these dreams people have access to their memories and a correct sense of their personal self. I had such a dream and it was a bit frightening. It disturbed my sense of reality. When writing about these dreams of being awake and their implications for philosophy, Bertrand Russell pointed out that we cannot prove that we are not having such a dream now.[9] That is an important clue. Some dreams are so real, so vivid, so veridical, that we can confuse them with reality. But the point is that what we take to be reality is a kind of dream, in that the perceptions are created by the brain from sensory input.

Paying attention to dreaming, we can observe several notable clues. While dreaming, the brain in some manner disconnects from the motor system, so that while dreaming of running we don't flail about and injure ourselves. (Sleepwalking is not a normal occurrence.) Also, people seldom report having painful sensations in their dreams. The sensations of taste and smell are rarely reported in dreams. Access to memory during dreaming seems to be enhanced. People often include long-forgotten events in their dreams. And lastly, the sense of agency is usually absent in dreams. That is, the dream usually has some bizarre plot that the dreamer witnesses rather than controls.[10]

With practice, people can train themselves to have some degree of control over their dreams. This practice, called lucid dreaming,[11] a state between sleeping and wakefulness, is also being investigated with the tools of brain research.[12] Lucid dreams are good clues, because in them the dreamer retains some sense of self, yet realizes that the seemingly real environment around them is not real. But this, of course, is the same point that Socrates is making in his conversation with Glaucon. What we see around us in waking life is a kind of dream, one created by the brain from the input of the senses.

Hallucinations, a type of waking dream, can also provide clues. When there is a problem with the brain, people can experience hallucinations, but they can occur for other reasons. Sometimes a patient must be awake during brain surgery to allow the surgeon to ascertain the function of the area around a tumor. While the brain is exposed it's surface can be directly stimulated by a mild electric current. In certain sections of the naked brain this causes the awake patient to have visual experiences, a vivid recreations of past events. Patients in certain brain operations must be kept awake so the surgeon can test where to make the cut be sure it isn't severing a critical function like speech. In this case there is an input (the electric buzz). However, that input is not really creating the imagery, but triggering a stored event. Again, the brain creates a virtual reality all by itself.

A recent addition to the tools of the brain researcher is transcranial magnetic stimulation (TMS), which blasts the cranium with a brief but intense magnetic pulse.[13] This technique has the benefit of not requiring the brain to be exposed. Patients in brain surgery are often quite ill, but magnetic pulse volunteers can be healthy and thus results are not clouded by pathology. In physics class we learn that a rapidly changing magnetic field will be accompanied by an electric field. You can feel this easily if you have a strong magnet. A sheet of copper is nonmagnetic—bou can't pick it up with a magnet—but if you quickly move the magnet across the copper without touching it, you can feel a drag.[14] The drag is caused by an induced electric current in the copper (which imitates a magnet of opposite polarity). In TMS a much stronger magnetic pulse is used. When it penetrates the skin and skull it induces a weak electric current in the brain. When this is done, some subjects report having remarkable experiences. Depending on which area of the brain is targeted, visual or auditory hallucinations can be elicited. Although these hallucinations are not nearly as detailed as those reported with direct stimulation of brain tissue, the TMS technique shows that our brain is creating what we experience.

Drugs and Anesthetics

Another clue to the brain's role in our conscious display is the effect of drugs. Many drugs are classified as hallucinogens, LSD being one of the more researched. How does LSD work on the body? Sensory signals are passed from receptor cells to nerve cells (neurons), which pass the signals to other nerve cells on a path to various brain areas. The nerves do not directly touch each other, but are separated by small gaps, the synapses. Chemicals are released by one neuron at the synapse and may eventually trigger the next neuron to continue the signal. LSD apparently can influence the chemistry in the gap. It lowers the threshold for the passing of the signal. Say we are looking at a clear blue sky. The blue receptors of the retina are active, but the red and green ones are below threshold and we see a uniform blue expanse. With LSD present, nerves may fire with little or no initiating signal. The visual area of the brain may now be getting signals from the red and green receptors as well as the blue. There is a part of the brain whose function is to make sense of incoming signals as best as it can. Instead of seeing a normal blue sky, now the sky has reds and greens, constantly changing, perhaps swirling with patterns gleaned from random noise. This is a chemically altered state of mind...a hallucination.

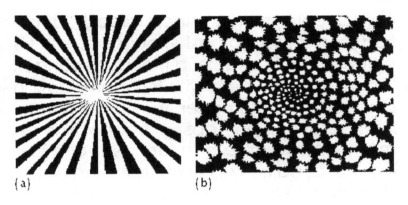

(a) (b)

Fig (a) Funnel and (b) spiral tunnel hallucinations generated by LSD.[15]

Even extremely small amounts of LSD, micrograms, can have a big effect on perception, providing a good clue as to the chemical basis of consciousness. Chemicals can change the way the brain creates its virtual reality, but there is no reason to believe they enhance the perception of what is out there.

Other drugs affect perception via different brain alterations. I'm thinking here of alcohol, laughing gas, and marijuana. These drugs seem to affect the brain's connection to memory. In the normal state, objects enter consciousness already identified, connected to past experience—this is a tree, a chair, a table, a friend, a stranger. When drugs interfere with this identification process, the interpreter will force a new interpretation, perhaps a bizarre one. A mildly altered state can feel fresh or relaxing, but a radically altered state can cause dangerous situation to be incorrectly registered (misjudging one's speed while driving). Again, the effect of these drugs shows the connection of consciousness to chemical activity. Our consciousness is not immediately connected to the external world, but is mediated by much chemistry.

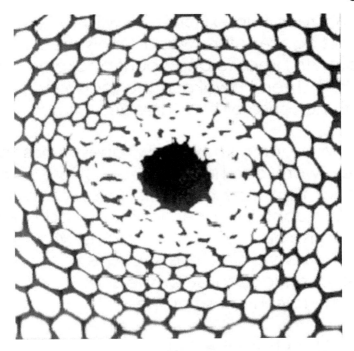

Honeycomb hallucination generated by marijuana.[16]

A final clue to the brain/chemical/con-sciousness connection is the effect of sleep-ing pills and anesthetics. Both induce sleep, loss of consciousness, but anesthetized brains will remain asleep even through the trauma of surgery. This is not an alteration of consciousness, but its complete elimination. I recall an experience with tonsilitis 60 years ago. As ether was administered, I was asked to breathe and count backward: 10, 9, 8, 7...Then I awoke in the recovery room with no sense of the passage of time.

We don't know how anesthetics do their work on the brain, but there is no doubt that they do work. The fact that a small quantity of chemical can lead to loss of consciousness, which returns when the chemical wears off, is strong evidence of the chemical/consciousness link and the brain's role in consciousness.

Clues from the Eye

At this moment I assume you are reading a book. Were you to eliminate all the light illuminating the book (say by taking it into a dark closet), you would no longer see the book. A more or less convincing proof that you need light to see. Reflection of light off the book enters the pupil of the eye. Our eye does not see the book; it responds to the light that enters the eye. More correctly, this light excites rod and cone cells in the retina, which trigger signals along one or more paths of the optic nerve connecting the eye to the brain. It is these chemical signals reaching the visual areas of the brain that we "see." We don't see the book, but rather create some impression of the book from the information carried on these chemical signals.

These signals can be detected by inserting a tiny wire into the nerve and eavesdropping on its activity. What is detected? Millisecond long bursts of low voltage repeated numerous times, separated by a few milliseconds. Electric spikes of chemical discharge travel, rather slowly (about the speed of a car), along the nerves. The frequency of these discharges is billions of times lower than the frequency of the light that triggers the retinal cells. The signals do not imitate the light that initiates them. The nerve signals coming from red-sensitive cells are the same as those coming from blue-sensitive cells. The brain adds red to the scene when the signals from those red-sensitive cells reach the appropriate part of the brain. The brain has no direct connection to the world outside itself. It is connected by the signals from the sense receptors. All it knows are those signals, from which the brain generates an internal world.

Since the late 1800s, it has been known that "light" is an electromagnetic (EM) phenomenon—pulses of rapidly oscillating electric and magnetic fields. But the bursts of EM energy are not colored. These bursts, photons, can excite certain retinal cells, which in turn excite the brain, which produces the sensation of colored light. In trying to write sentences like the previous one, we encounter a problem with our language. The word "light" can refer to the external physical phenomenon and to the internal experience of brightness. With an updated understanding, a sentence such as, "Light is not light" can have meaning. Or, "Red light is not red." It is the brain that adds light and color to our world. There is no light or color "out there." Light and color are "in here" sensations. We each color our own world, and philosophers are fond of pointing out that there is no way for us to prove that we all have the same color experience. When I talk to people about this color stuff, most have no trouble accepting the argument and many say they thought of it independently as children. But it is not enough to convince them of WYSIRY.

Some people ask about prisms: Don't prisms have the ability to separate light into colors? Not really. When we say light we usually mean sunlight or lamp light, which is produced by a hot source that emits electromagnetic energy with a blend of different frequencies. As these various frequencies pass through the prism, they are bent (refracted) at different angles depending on their frequency and on the material of which the prism is composed (diamond bends light more than glass). Thus light is separated into its frequency components. Only when these frequencies enter the eye, exciting the retina and brain, do we experience the (internal) sensation of color. Again, the color is not out there, but in here. WYSIRY.

A Clue from the Blind Spot

Close your right eye, and look out with just the left. We usually don't pay attention to the extreme edges of our vision. On the right side of your field of view you can see the left side of your nose. At the top is your eyebrow; a few hairs might protrude into your view. There is not much at the left, but the bottom is defined by the upper part of the cheek. Sometimes the lips can be seen, particularly if they are moving. The view from the right eye is similar but reversed. When both eyes are open, there is a partial overlap of the two views. Roughly the middle third of full vision is covered by both eyes; the left and right thirds are covered by only one eye. In each field of view there is a kind of dead spot, the blind spot, due to the lack of rods or cones in the place where the optic nerve enters and leaves the retina.[17] When light is focused on the retina, this spot produces no output. The spot is blind. The blind spots are in this central third of our field of vision.

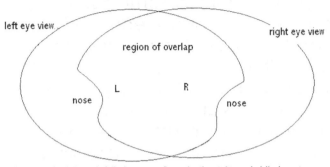

L marks the left eye's blind spot   R marks the right eye's blind spot

The two fields of view, left and right, and their overlap, are illustrated above. The blind spot of the left eye is labeled by an L, and that of the right eye by an R.

In the overlap region, the left eye can cover the blind spot of the right eye and vice versa, so in our internal display there seems to be no missing information. To find your blind spot, try this simple exercise. Close your left eye and hold the book up in front of your face with your right eye fixed on the **R** below:

R   **L**

Move the book closer to and farther from your face until at some distance (about one foot) the **L** disappears from view. Of course the **L** is still there, but at the proper distance its image falls on a spot of the retina that has no light sensors. With one eye closed there is always a blind spot in the field of vision, but the brain compensates for it. The size of the spot is about six degrees, and it is located about 15 degrees to the right of where the right eye is focused. Light reflected from an object in that area falls on a dead spot of the retina and hence sends no information to the brain.[18] The brain goes ahead and constructs a representation as best it can without that information. I read a story about King Charles II who, after he learned of the blind spot, would amuse himself during boring court proceedings by "beheading" his subjects. With his right eye open and focused on a head, he would shift his gaze slowly to the left until the head disappeared.

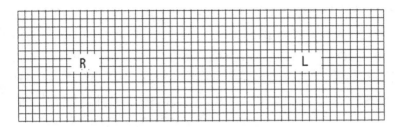

Now close your left eye, focus on the **R**, and try the blind spot experiment on this grid. Notice how the grid heals itself. When the **L** disappears, there will not be a "hole" in the grid pattern. The pattern appears complete. Your brain has taken care of the problem.

There is a similar blind spot for the left eye (focus on the **L**, and the **R** can be made to vanish). With both eyes open, there is no blind spot apparent because of the overlap in the field of vision. The missing information of each eye is provided by information from the other eye.

There is another very interesting visual phenomenon that you can experience with the grid above. Stare at the **L** with both eyes open. After a few seconds, the

R will disappear and the grid will seem to heal. Any small movement of your eyes will refresh the **R**, so keep your focus steady on the **L**. In this case, the distance from your eyes to the grid does not seem to matter. This is an important clue in our quest for information pointing to the brain's role in creating our brainscape.

For more blind spot experiments, you can turn to *Phantoms in the Brain*[19] where you can test your blind spot on several more advanced tests, which reveal subtle features of the brain's attempt to compensate for the information missing in that area.

Once you learn to play with your blind spot, you can see what an excellent clue this is to WYSIRY. Our vision has a hole in it but we learn to ignore it. Our internal recreation of the outside world seems complete, but the blind spot points to a hole in the illusion.

Double Vision

If you have normal vision, and are observing the scene in front of you, it is common to feel you are looking at the world directly. There seems to be one world out there, and you are seeing it. But look closely. Focus on some object at middle distance, say five feet, but pay attention to an object nearer to you. It will appear double! Objects in the far distance (when you are fixed at middle distance) will also appear double. In fact, the only object that is single in appearance is the one on which you are focused. All others are doubled, with the separation of the twin images growing as their distance from your object of focus increases. If you are seeing one world directly how can it be double? The illusion of one world is so strong that you still may not see it, so try this easy procedure.

Hold up a finger of your left hand a foot from your eyes, and focus your vision on it. Remain focused on that finger and hold up a finger from your right hand a foot behind it. The far finger appears double. Two images of the finger can be seen, separated by about the distance between your eyes. Moving the far finger to three feet will increase the separation between the twin images.

Now focus on the far finger instead of the near finger. The far finger appears single, but the near finger is doubled. If we have two working eyes, we always see double. We don't ordinarily notice this doubling, because the brain incorporates the left and right views into a convincing representation of the outside. The real (outside) world is single. Our image of it is double. The double image is not real. What we see is our image of reality, WYSIRY. What you see is really you.

Crossing your eyes to look at the tip of your nose will double the world to the extreme. So extreme that some people are a bit disoriented, sickened, by this experiment. Thus, the cross-eyed trick is not very useful in demonstrating doubling. A bit better is to try pressing gently with a finger on the corner of your eyeball (or both eyeballs) while your eyes are open. Again there will be doubling. For me, the images not only shift but also rotate slightly and disturb the sense of what is vertical.

All this image-making takes place in the brain. What you see, which appears to be in front of you, outside of you, is actually taking place inside your brain. It is a brainscape, not a landscape. We know it is a brain phenomenon, because injuries to the brain can disturb the image-making whereas injuries to a foot or liver or kidney or tongue do not. The brain is the organ of perception.

Clues from Op Art

With your eyes closed, apply a moderate steady pressure to both eyes. I don't recommend doing this too often, as the pressure can't be good for the eyes. In a short while some remarkable patterns will emerge. The pressure evidently fires up the receptors in the retina, which fire up the optic nerve, which creates patterns that can be quite interesting. Here is an appearance totally generated by the eye-brain system. The visual patterns, called phosphenes, do not appear to be in the eye. Like most images they seem to be outside.

Back in the 60s, the Op Art movement began making use of optical illusions in visual art. Some Op Art paintings imitate the patterns seen when applying pressure to the eyes. The patterns are interesting because they reveal something about how the cells of the retina are ordered. The patterns are not anything we have seen in the real world, but we all relate to them because we all have similar retinas. I am saying this is a clue because the pressure patterns appear to be out there but they are obviously in here.

Fig. a. Phosphene produced by deep binocular pressure on the eyeballs.[20]

Related to this is the phenomenon reported by the early astronauts of seeing sparkles and flashes of light. Even with their eyes closed they saw these brief bursts that seemed to be outside their bodies. It was decided that cosmic ray particles were passing through their brains and stimulating momentary visual sparks as brain cells were being destroyed.[21] We are fairly well insulated from cosmic rays (actually high-speed atomic nuclei) by our atmosphere, although a couple times a year I seem to detect a similar phenomenon in my visual field. It appears as a brief flash of color, usually not in the center of my field vision. These flashes are not something that exists in the external world—they are anomalies of the visual system.

Clues from Eye Movement

Sit still in a chair and observe your surroundings. As your eyes scan the scene, looking at one detail or another, the sense is of a fixed, unmoving landscape. We can look left, right, up, or down but the landscape does not seem to move. However, we know that as the eye scans the scene, the image on the retina is being changed quite drastically. The brain compensates for this changing input and displays instead a stable scene. The brain must be executing an enormous amount of computation to achieve this.

However, if we quickly look left, right, left, right, the brain is hard-pressed to maintain the fiction of a fixed world, and the image gets scrambled. This can make some people feel a bit queasy in the stomach. The world is not scrambled. Our brainscape is scrambled. This is a clue that what we are seeing is not the world in itself, but our picture of it.

What if we stop our eyes from scanning and fixate on a point, say a dark spot or a bright spot? Stare at the spot and try not let your focus move. If you drift off the spot, bring your focus back. This may take a little practice. Stillness can be achieved by anesthetizing the ocular muscles, but this exercise is close enough and worth the effort.

This is not an easy exercise because the eye is never completely still. The eye makes small jumps, called saccades or microsaccades, three to five times each second. Saccadic movements shift the image on the retina, which is necessary to "refresh" the vision. If the image on the retina is fixed, the scene will fade in a few seconds. The saccade restores the image. Experimenters have made special contact lenses that project a fixed image on the retina, thus, eliminating the refreshment of those tiny saccadic movements. Subjects fitted with the device report that their vision rapidly fades—not just becoming dimmer but entirely vanishing. Light is still being focused on the retina, but the cells have become accustomed to the illumination and no longer send signals. This is a very good clue that what you see is not a direct view of the real world.

With a little practice and some patience you can get a feeling for this fading effect. Stare at a spot intently without blinking (blinking is a kind of refreshing) and you will see the image begin to fade. This may take a minute or two. To me, the scene starts to look like an impressionistic pastel. Patches of color tend to whiten, while the edges of the patches hold their color better. Consider this situation: adjacent groups of retinal cones (the cells that detect color) are being bathed in red and blue colored light (represented here by white and black circles). Of course the light is not colored, but rather of certain frequency ranges.

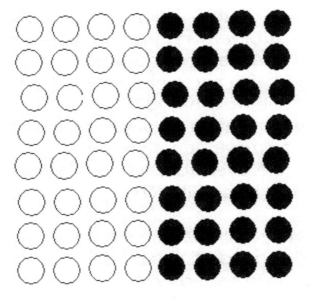

Tiny movements of the head and eye, will minutely shift the border between the color patches. Most of the cells will not "change color," except those at the border. The border cells will flip color and be refreshed and hence emphasize the borderline. Inevitably a blink will occur and set you back a bit, but stay with it and soon, with practice in holding still, your vision will fade. The world fades away, again revealing it as an image you see and not a direct view of something external.

If you do this fixation exercise outdoors, where a breeze can cause subtle movements in leaves, the movements stand out. As I do this in my front yard, my gaze fixed on a stone wall, the wall fades, but undulating plants remain clearly in my consciousness. The movement stands out. This makes sense, the eye/brain system is sensitive to motion. It helps with survival.

I've read that some creatures, like frogs and flies, are particularly tuned to motion. It is difficult to swat a fly with your hand but if you approach the fly very slowly by sliding your finger toward it, often it will ignore the finger and even climb on. Perhaps a fly (or a frog) only sees things if they are moving.

> The frog does not seem to see or, at any rate, is not concerned with the detail of stationary parts of the world around him. He will starve to death surrounded by food if it is not moving.[22]

What a strange consciousness where things disappear when they stop. Damasio[23] writes of people with damage to a certain area of the brain who do not see motion. An approaching car appears to be a succession of still views, with the car becoming larger in each view. The sense of motion is missing in this dysfunction. It is dangerous for such people to cross the street, as they cannot correctly judge motion. They report that even filling a glass with water is difficult.

We are like the frog in that we cannot see movement if it is too slow. We know the minute hand on a clock is moving, but even close attention does not evoke the sense of something moving. The same is true for shadows of objects in sunlight. Locate the tip of a shadow and place a small stone there. Usually you won't notice the shadow shifting, but in five minutes it will have moved so the stone is no longer at the tip.[24] The point is: things may be moving in the world outside but we are not sensitive to all movement. We have our limitations.

On the other hand we can create a sense of motion where there is none. Films are a succession of still pictures projected at

24 frames per second.[25] This is fast enough to create the illusion of continuous motion. The illusion is very good, of course. Most of us are completely taken in by the effect as we watch the faux movement on the screen. Nothing is moving, but try remembering that as you view the action. We are easily fooled into accepting the apparent motion as real.

If you are willing to put up with some flicker, far less than 24 frames per second will produce the illusion of movement. I'm thinking of flip books with simple animated figures on successive pages. Using your thumb you can flip the pages, rather slowly even, and see the figures dance.

Clues from the Strobe Effect

Electrical energy is delivered to our homes as alternating current which alternates 60 times each second (50 in the UK). This alternation does not affect incandescent lightsbulbs very much as they produce light when their filament gets hot and glows. The electricity goes off and on 60 times a second, but the temperature of the filament stays pretty constant so the light is fairly steady. Fluorescent lighting works on a different principle[26] and suffers from more severe ups and downs in light output. Some people can detect fluorescent flicker, particularly in peripheral vision, and find it annoying. This type of lighting, strobing on and off at 60 hertz, can create a dangerous illusion.

Sometimes machinery, such as a lathe or fan, that is powered by 60 hertz electricity can appear to be stopped when actually it is moving. Say the machine rotates 60 times per second while it is illuminated by a fluorescent light that is flickering 60 times each second. The rotating part will be in the same position each time the light flashes on, and it will appear to be still. That is why such fluorescent lighting is not permitted in a workplace using such equipment. In other circumstances this effect can be useful. If you want to inspect a fan blade for damage while it is operating, you can synchronize a strobe light to the fan's rotation rate and it will "stop" for your viewing.

Auto mechanics use this trick to look at timing marks on the fan belt of cars (at least they once did).

When I was teaching, I could always get the attention of my students by setting the lab faucet to drip at a steady rate and shining a strobe light on the falling drops. At the proper sync rate, the "drop" appears to be floating...frozen in mid-fall. The word "drop" is in quotes because each flash illuminates a different drop, but the illusion is of a string of drops suspended beneath the faucet. A slight shift of the strobe rate can cause them to look as if they are floating up into the faucet. A similar illusion can be seen on TV when a moving car is displayed. The wheels sometimes appear to be going backward when the rotation rate nearly matches the TV screen's refresh rate. The point is, our visual system is easily fooled. Our vision has been pruned by natural selection to help our survival, not to deal with the unusual situation of illumination by strobe lights.

I learned about the danger of strobes quite innocently in the 60s. As a graduate student I had access to a very bright strobe with a short (one-millionth of a second) flash that could be varied by turning a knob. Working alone one night, I noticed that when the flash, which was essentially white, illuminated a plain white paper, colors seemed to wash over the paper. I held the paper to my eyes and illuminated it from the rear. I could see colored patterns. The flash was bright so I closed my eyes. Even with my eyes closed the patterns of color were still there. At around 10 flashes per second, the patterns were most intricate and captivating. Patterns changed one into another, slowly enough to observe but too quickly to recall. It was fascinating, bewitching really. But I was alone in the otherwise dark lab and I got a little uneasy and terminated the experience. The next day I was invited to dinner with friends and thought they would be interested in seeing this.

I brought the strobe along, and after dessert I told them of my experience and everyone wanted to try. All were fascinated by what they saw, but one woman in particular was enraptured. We forgot about her as we continued to chat—then suddenly she went into a seizure, just as I had seen years earlier with an epileptic person. She stopped her uncontrolled movements in a couple of minutes, but we observers continued to be frightened. She fell quietly asleep, and when she awoke an hour later, she asked for the strobe—with no memory of what had happened. Her husband said this had never happened to her before. I've never tried the experiment again after that evening.

Afterwards, I learned that many strobe lights carry a warning about the possibility of triggering such seizures. But other more common situations can induce seizures: driving in a tunnel at 25 miles per hour with lights spaced a yard apart; or driving down a sun lit road with regularly spaced trees shadowing the roadway will simulate a strobe of 10 flashes per second. These situations are known to trigger seizures in susceptible people.

In December of 1997, a Pokemon cartoon aired on Japanese television. It showed a cartoon explosion followed by a mere five seconds of flickering red and blue lights. In that brief exposure, 685 children were triggered into epileptic seizure and 13,000 were affected in some lesser way. Later tests on a few of the affected children showed that a black-and-white version of the cartoon did notcause seizure, and that it was the red/blue changes that caused the problem. A new color-sensitive form of epilepsy was revealed. Since then some countries have passed regulations to prevent this from happening again.

What could be happening when the strobe induces the sensation of colored patterns illuminating white paper? There is no patten in the illumination or the white sheet of paper. All the rods and cones in the retina are firing at once when the light pulse (which is very short) is over. The retina is dark for a tenth of a second. The optic nerve must be sending short, sharp shocks to the visual center of the brain—10 pulses each second. The nerve pathways from the retinal cells to the brain cells might all be slightly different, so the various signals do not arrive at the brain at the same time. In addition to receiving the incoming pulses, the brain itself is sending pulses around within itself to do its work (such as the alpha and beta waves). Somehow the strong, pulsating light signals of the strobe interfere with the normal operation of the brain to create these captivating hallucinations. The brain gets confused, and part of this confusion is to attribute changing color and pattern to visual input. It is interesting to us because it is us. But the interference can be dangerous. Don't try this at home.

I was reintroduced to the strobe effect when I came to live in California a decade or so after my horrific strobe scare. I was playing tennis under the lights for the first time. Some kind of fluorescent lighting was used, which, like all such lights, was strobing at 60 times per second. I couldn't detect any flicker in the lighting but the sight of the tennis ball was amazing. A ball can advance a foot or two in the time between flashes, and that is what I saw—a tennis ball jumping a foot at a time across the court. At first, laughing at the sight, I couldn't hit the ball, but I quickly adapted. Now only with special effort, keeping the strobe effect in mind, can I somewhat recapture that jumping ball effect. Watching tennis on TV with the screen refresh rate about the same, you can see the ball, elongated by blur, skip from one position to another. Most of the time, not thinking about our vision, we fall into the illusion of seeing the ball in continuous motion.

Clues from the Phi Effect

Motion pictures create the illusion of motion by displaying a succession of still images. The first patent for a device (called the zoopraxiscope) to do this was awarded to William Lincoln in 1867. But it was a psychologist, Max Wertheimer, who studied the phenomenon and dubbed it *phi*. The following paragraph, describing an important experiment, is from *Consciousness Explained* by Daniel Dennett:

In the simplest case, if two or more small spots separated by as much as 4 degrees of visual angle are briefly lit in rapid succession, a single spot will seem to move back and forth...The philosopher Nelson Goodman had asked [experimenter] Kolers whether the phi phenomenon persisted if the two illuminated spots were different in color, and if so, what happened to the color of "the" spot as "it" moved? Would the illusion of motion disappear, to be replaced by two separately flashing spots? Would an illusory "moving" spot gradually change from one color to another...? Two different colored spots [red and green] were lit for 150msec each (with a 50msec interval); the first spot seemed to begin moving and then change color abruptly in the middle of its illusory passage toward the second location.

What is remarkable to me is not the appearance of an oscillating spot changing color from such a simple setup but the experimenter's claim that it can be evoked in a subject on the first cycle. A spot lights red, then a spot lights green, but the subject reports seeing a single spot moving, say right to left, and changing color in mid-course.

Think about this for a moment. If these reports are correct, the subject sees a red spot, but before the green spot is flashed, the subject "sees" the red spot moving and turning green. I found these results hard to accept, so I talked a friend into programming his computer to simulate the red/green spot experiment.[27] Alas, we could not reproduce the effect. Perhaps the spot brightness or timing was off. I trust that the experimental evidence offered is correct. I wish I could have "seen" it with my own eyes.

I mention the color phi effect here because I think it is an excellent clue as to how we construct our virtual reality. The interesting part of the color phi effect is how it focuses our attention on the flow of time in consciousness. Only after the second light, the green one, flashes on and excites the retina, and after the optic nerve signal reaches the brain, can the brain begin to form the illusion of the red light moving and turning to green. But what appears in consciousness is red, red-moving, red-turning-green, green-moving, green. The time sequence presented to consciousness and reported by the subjects, is a time illusion. The actual order is red, green, then some brain interpolation. Of course, no light is moving, but in addition to that illusion, the events sensed by the subject could not have occurred in the reported sequence... there is a time illusion as well.

You can experience the color Phi effect for yourself quite easily by visiting the website http://www.socsci.uci.edu/cogsci/personnel/hoffman/vi6 and choosing Phi Applet. Then you can select the color—red/blue is good—and the speed to see for yourself if there is some sense of a single dot moving rather than two dots alternately blinking. For me, there was a feeling of movement, but the sense of blinking was dominant. I had no illusion that a dot was moving and changing color. Perhaps it will be different for you. There are several other good illusions on the site, and they certainly reinforce the suggestion that our brains can represent motion when actually nothing is moving.

Clues from the Third Dimension

Three-dimensional vision is perhaps the best clue to what we might call the internality of vision—that the phenomenon of vision, what we see, is a brain process. When we have our eyes open and look around we see objects in their full glory. The table in front of me looks solid, it has volume, and it has depth along with height and width. The Greek word "stereos," meaning "solid" or "firm," is used to describe this quality of three dimensional vision—stereoscopic vision. It gives us a sense of things filling a volume of space, of being solid, of being real.

Three-D vision also locates objects in the space around us. Some things are close, some far, some in between. This sense of space can be quite vast, populated with stars, clouds, mountains, houses, trees, chairs, knees, and the tip of one's nose. What you may not have noticed is that this stereoscopic effect requires both eyes. To see in 3-D, you need to use two eyes.[28] You might try closing one eye, and perhaps things still look solid to you; you will still have a sense of near and far. This one-eyed vision is not true 3-D vision, but the brain's best shot at representing the world with the information at hand ("at eye" might be a better phrase). There are all sorts of clues the brain uses to reconstruct depth when information from only one eye is available. Actually many people have difficulty seeing correctly in three dimensions because one eye is dominant. They cannot, without training, see the depth in those stereo pairs that slip into a stereopticon (3-D viewer). Such people probably have poor hand/eye coordination.

Most of the time our field of view is filled with familiar things, things we can identify. Now I am sitting on my patio. I see a glass, a chair, a car, a house. The glass is visually bigger than the chair, but I "know" it is actually smaller, so it must be much closer to me than the chair. The chair is visually bigger than the car and house so it must be closer. There is a slight haze in the air, making distant objects more hazy than others. This helps in me locate them on the landscape (the brainscape). The breeze moves some plants to and fro (the closer ones), but others seem to move hardly at all (the distant ones) even though they are probably moving just as much. The chair overlaps the car, the car overlaps the house...more distance clues. Slight color changes (distant objects are bluer), loss of texture information, shadow overlap, etc. provide clues that the brain uses to simulate the sense of depth, but true 3-D requires two eyes.

Two eyes provide the brain with two slightly different views of the external world—two points of view. Close one eye and open the other, left, right, left, right, etc. You can see a jump in the scene. Particularly large jumps occur for nearby objects, while distant objects hardly shift at all. The brain, in ways that are just beginning to be understood, uses the information from these two views to create our familiar 3-D image of the world. Perhaps the clearest illustration of this are the stereograms introduced by Julez[29] in the 1960s. I once programmed my PC (in Basic programming language) to generate stereograms but the stereograms below are taken from the Internet.[30]

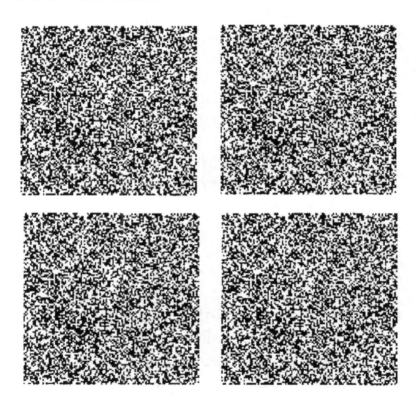

To view them in 3-D, concentrate on the top pair, hold the book about a foot in front of your eyes. Slightly cross your eye so you see three squares. Concentrate on the center square (which is actually the overlap of two images), and in a few seconds the 3-D image should appear. You will see a small square floating above the background. Shifting to the lower pair, which is the reverse of the upper pair, you will see the smaller square depressed behind a surrounding border. Here there is no hint of the size of the raised square except by a comparison of the two views. No haze or overlap will help you.

To create squares like these, make a 100 x 100 grid and randomly assign black or white to each of the cells in the left square. To make the right square, copy the outer twenty-five cells of the left square, but fill in the inside square by shifting the corresponding cells of the left inner square to the right by five cells. (Shifting the inner square to the left will create the appearance of a raised inner square.)

Inspecting either square by itself, you can't tell that there is a raised or depressed square in the center. Each square is essentially a random, salt and pepper, grid pattern. But the brain can take the two images and construct a 3-D image from them—an image that does not exist anywhere in the external world. It exists only in the virtual world of our brainscape. This sense of a small square above the border is true 3-D...there are no visual clues other than the stereo reconstruction. This is what the brain can do with two eyes. Actually the brain is extremely good at constructing the 3-D image. Even if one image is 10% larger than the other, or rotated 10 degrees, the brain will still do its trick.

I have described the cross-eyed method of viewing the stereograms above, in which the left eye views the right image and the right eye views the left. There is another method that you might find easier. Hold the book very close to the eyes, so the left image is in front of the left eye and the right image is in front of the right eye. Slowly pull the book away from the eyes until you can focus. Now the left eye sees the left image and the right eye sees the right. Of course now you will see the square depressed instead of raised when viewing the first stereo pair.

If you want to play with 3-D, it is very easy to make your own stereograms. Using your favorite camera take a shot of some scene then move the camera about three inches (the typical interocular distance) and take another photo from the new point of view. When printed, the photos can be viewed as a stereo pair. Actually, a good rule of thumb for the distance you shift between shots is about 1 to 20. For a subject 60 inches away, move three inches. For a subject 60 feet away, move three feet. You can ask a friend to sit unmoving for a few seconds and take a good 3-D portrait with a 3 inch move. Once, while in an airplane, I saw an unusual cloud formation maybe 20 miles away. I waited 6 seconds (about a mile) between shots to get an excellent 3-D look at clouds. Ordinarily clouds are so far away that we cannot, with our three inch eye separation, see them three-dimensionally—our eyes are too close together to reconstruct the image in 3-D. A good stereo shot of the Grand Canyon was taken by moving 300 feet along the rim. When objects in the landscape are beyond 100 feet away we put them in our brainscape as a flat background scenery.[31] I'm looking at a mountain through my office window and it looks like a wall, rather than gradually sloping ground leading to the peak.

You can do some amusing exercises with your 3-D vision. Find some repeated pattern in wallpaper, carpeting, floor tiles, or a chain link fence and view it with slightly crossed eyes. The pattern will seem to float above the plane where it once was. This can happen accidently, say when you turn a corner and a fence is suddenly in front of you, and your eyes are slightly crossed when they focus. The fence appears closer than it is. View the image below while slightly crossing your eyes. After your eyes refocus, the image of the fence will appear to be above the plane of the page.

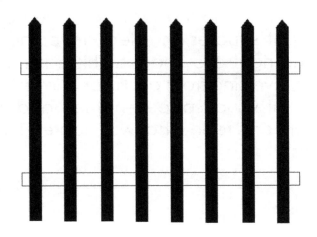

Clues from 3-D Inversion

Related to the Julez stereograms, which show a small square either above or below the border of a larger square, is another revealing example. In the image below the ellipses in the far left and far right squares are the same. The center square contains similar ellipses placed at slightly different horizontal positions within the border. This imitates the different left and right views of a 3-D scene. View the left and center squares with crossed eyes as a stereo pair. The ellipse at the lower right seems closest and the one at the upper right seems farthest. Now do the same with the center and right squares, in effect, reversing the left and right eye images. This has the effect of reversing front and rear. It inverts the apparent visual space—not left and right but front and rear. What was nearest is now farthest.

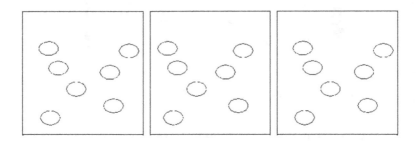

The space we perceive around us is our own creation. Our brain places the objects it discerns in the brainscape according to the information it receives. One of the strongest cues for spatial location is binocular disparity—the difference in the scene as seen by each eye.

The brain creates a sense of tremendous space surrounding our bodies. There may be tremendous space around us, but like our friend bound in the cave, we see only a secondary shadow of that space. On the cave wall, space is flattened into a 2-D shadow show, and the actual spatial separations appear as different fuzziness in the shadows. Our representation of space is much better than a shadow, so much better that it takes some thought to loosen the grip of the effect. These little images above show us how we are capable of creating a sense of space where there is none, and show how we can reverse near and far simply by "switching eyes." This is a tremendous clue that we too are in a cave, an organic cave of the skull, and that we are doing our best to get a sense of what is outside. We fashion our brainscape from the information supplied by our senses. We all are so good at doing this that we usually don't realize that we are not seeing the world directly. WYSIRY.

Clues from Observing Space

Along with color, sound, smell, taste, and touch, the brain creates a sense of space and time. Careful observation can reveal some peculiarities in our internal display of space and time. Notice how we are selectively sensitive to the vertical dimension. Acrophobia, fear of heights, is a fairly common phobia, but few people have a fear of width. Pay attention to a long stick, say an eight-foot two-by-four. Laying on the ground it does not seem nearly a big as it does when raised to be vertical. (This is similar to that "stovepipe hat" illusion: the brim is as wide as the hat is tall, but the hat appears to be taller than it is wide.) I am quite tall, 6' 6', and often see people do a double take when I stand up. I might be taller than someone by only a few inches, say the width of a hand, but to them I seem extremely tall.

Our brain does weird things with space when we are next to a large, slowly moving object. Standing next to a train as it leaves the station, we often feel that it is we who are drifting in the opposite direction. Some people even fell ill just being near a large thing. Not just a long thing, a train, but something also tall, like an ocean liner.

The very size of it can throw off our space perception. People peering down into the Grand Canyon, nearly a mile deep, can get a similar feeling of disorientation.

Our brain takes the virtually infinite space around us and makes it into a virtual display that fits in our skull. This requires a subtle distortion of parallel lines, for example, which we can notice if it is pointed out. Below is an intriguing quote from Steve Lehar's website:[32]

> For the most part perception is indirect, we view the world through the medium of conscious experience. But there is one, and only one entity that we do see directly, and that is the representational mechanism itself, the inside of our own brain. **The volume of space we perceive around us is a data structure in our physical brain, and the primal color qualia with which that world is painted are different states of the physical mechanism of our own physical brain....**But then how come things in the distance look smaller? Perspective is something

that happens in your eye, not out in the world! In the real street things in the distance are not actually smaller, all the houses are exactly the same size. It is only on your retina that the farther ones appear smaller. And the image on your retina is only a flat 2-D image. This world out here is 3-D, but it has perspective. So is it the world itself? Or is it the image on the retina?

You should read Lehar's Cartoon Epistemology for his unique take on how our spatial display reveals that it is a display and not an immediate viewing of external reality.

Clues from Afterimages

Afterimages are simple clues to the operation of our visual system. For the simplest case, fix your gaze on a dark object hanging on a white wall. After 20 seconds shift your gaze to a bare portion of the wall. The shape of the dark object will now appear on the white wall, but it will be brighter (whiter) than the white of the wall. While it lasts, the afterimage really appears to be on the wall, but because it moves when we move our eyes and also fades quickly, we are not fooled into thinking it is an image of something real. But at first, we may be deceived and think it is "out there" on the wall, not a result of our retinal cells recovering from fatigue.

You can also fixate on a brightly colored object, and then the afterimage will take on the complimentary color. The afterimage fades rapidly but gives a good clue as to how color is not in the external object but in our visual system. There is a fascinating website[33] where you can view hundreds of original optical illusions, many of which utilize color afterimages for their effect.

An interesting afterimage experiment is close at hand. Fixate on a 60-watt frosted light bulb (while it is on of course) for about a minute, then close your eyes, maybe even cover them with something dark, and pay attention to the intense afterimage. As it fades it will pass through a series of different colors, usually ending up with a beautiful blue color. This blue is not a color you have ever seen on a real object; it is a very internal color. If you have normal vision, you have three color receptors on your retina: red, green, and blue (RGB). But even a pure (single frequency) blue light from a laser will stimulate, to some extent, the red and green receptors. Thus the signal reaching the brain will be "blue" with some "red" and "green" added. (The "blue" in quotes refers to the electrochemical signal produced by the blue-sensitive retinal cells.) However, the "blue" of the afterimage is a pure "blue" because the red and green retinal cells apparently cease firing before the blue cells, which continue to produce some output. Thus the afterimage blue is a color you never can see in nature, and it reveals that it is we who create color.

With a little effort you can see an interesting afterimage by cutting out a dime-sized red circle and placing it on a gray background. Stare at the red circle for about 30 seconds and then remove the circle. A complimentary bluish circle will now be seen on the gray background. If you repeat the staring part of the demonstration and then look at a white background, the afterimage, still bluish, will now seem to be self-luminous, brighter than white.[34] This is a color that no natural object viewed in its reflected light can have. It is a supranatural color created by your visual system. Of course, no afterimage is a real event—all such images are brain-created phenomena—but this effect is interesting in that no natural object could be so colored.

A different kind of afterimage is set up when we fixate on a moving pattern for a while and then shift to a non-moving pattern. Stare at a rotating disk for a while, one with radial spokes, then shift focus to a stationary disk. It will appear to rotate in the opposite direction. I first noticed this effect[35] when viewing steady ripples coming onto a lake shore, then shifting focus to the land. The land appeared to move. A similar effect can be noticed after riding in a car and watching the road slide toward you. When the car comes to a stop the road still appears to move...away from you. A more active experiment: would be to just stand up and spin around with your eyes open. After you accommodate to the spinning, when you stop the room continues to spin... in the opposite direction.

What is the clue here? In all these cases, we see that although the image on the retina (after viewing a moving field) is not moving, there is an illusion of motion. The sense of something moving is being created by the brain even though there is no longer any motion. Keeping track of moving things is obviously useful to survival, but we can be fooled into tagging something with the "feeling of motion" when it is not moving. Actual moving things can trigger this "feeling of motion," but we can create a false tag under unusual circumstances.

Clues from Mirrors

Mirrors are so common that we may need to be reminded how effective they are at tricking the brain. In the entry of my home there is an eight-foot mirror, half that wide, which rests on the tile floor. Sometimes new visitors (and dogs too) have turned into the mirror as though it were a portal into another room. Mirrors, of course, reflect light into our eyes. The eyes then treat this reflected light the same as the direct light from the objects, forming a focused pattern on the retina that produces signals, via the optic nerve, to inform the brain. Our experience with mirrors has taught us that there is no space behind the mirror surface. Look into a mirror and you will see an obvious virtual reality informed by the reflected light. But—and here's the point—everything around the mirror, the walls, floor, etc., also reflects light into the eyes where the signals spark the brain in the same manner to create a grand illusion...of a room with a mirror. All of it is happening in your brain. [Note: I am not saying "*just* happening."]

A little aside: Most of us learn to recognize our own faces by looking in mirrors. But a mirror creates a parity inversion. If you have a mark on your left cheek, the face in the mirror has a mark on its right cheek. We see our face "reversed" in the mirror. Since most of us are not very symmetrical when we see our face "correctly" (as others see us) in a photograph we may feel the photo does not look like us...even though friends say it does. You can see yourself "correctly" by using two mirrors held at 90 degrees to each other, forming a corner. Now when you wink with your right eye, the image will blink its right eye.

Another aside: Most of the mirrors we use have the "silvering" on the rear surface (usually aluminum). Thus any object reflected is actually double, a strong (95%) reflection off the "silver" and a weak (5%) reflection off the outer glass surface. Look at a candle flame with a mirror. You will see a bright flame with a weak flame slightly shifted. Special front surface mirrors can be purchased and their reflections are remarkably sharp. However, they scratch easily and are hard to clean.

Magicians have used mirrors to produce illusions for centuries...and smoke to hide the mirrors. To say something is "smoke and mirrors" is to say, "it's an illusion." Other expressions from magic are "the hand is quicker than the eye" and "seeing is believing." Our visual system is easily fooled. We can easily be led into mistaking an illusion for reality. We do it all the time. Everything we see is an illusion, created by our brain from information (and misinformation) from the outside world. The task for us, we people of the cave, is to come to understand this. Follow the clues.

Clues from Optical Illusions

Thousands of optical illusions have been published and most of us have seen many of them. The classic ones have names. Here are a few.[36]

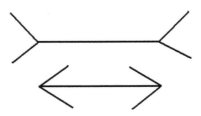

Muller-Lyer illusion: Two lines of equal length seem to be unequal when short lines are added.

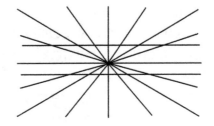

Herring illusion: Parallel lines appear to bulge when radiating lines are superimposed.

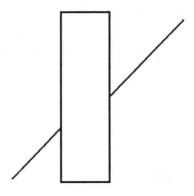

Poggendorf illusion: A rectangle appears to cover a straight line but the line is not straight.

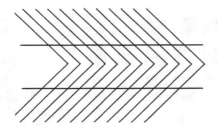

Zollner illusion: Two parallel lines appear to diverge.

Kanisza's triangle illusion: The (partial) circles seem to be under a triangle.

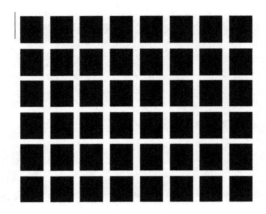

Ghost images: Faint gray dots seem to appear at the intersections.

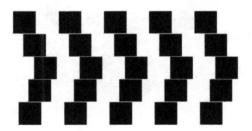

Café wall illusion: These squares appear to be non-parallel.

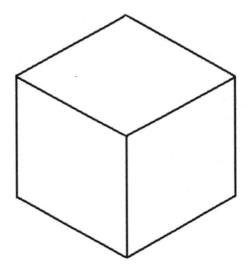

Finally, the famous Necker cube: This line drawing of a cube seems to "reverse."

The figure can be seen as box-like or as the corner of a room. It seems to flip from one to the other. You cannot see it both ways simultaneously. The cube figure is a flat, two-dimensional line drawing, but somehow the brain can tag it as being a cube or a corner.

These illusions serve to emphasize that what we see depends on the brain. We don't see parallel lines as parallel because of brain processes that are out of our control. Knowing they are actually parallel does not help us to see them that way. The Necker cube above is a hexagon with three radial lines. It lies flat on the page, but the visual system sees it as a 3-D figure above or below the plane of the paper. We always see the result of a brain process. WYSIRY.

Another common illusion can be seen when driving on a long level road on a hot, sunny day. We see what appears to be water on the road ahead, but as we approach the place where the water appeared to be, it is gone. But now a place farther ahead looks wet. This is the wet road illusion. Similar illusions in the desert cause people to see lakes in the distance. Of course we are really seeing skylight refracted upward off the road by a thin layer of hot air at the surface. Here we are fooled—not exactly by our brain, but by nature. But the point is that we have been fooled. The adage "seeing is believing" is true in the sense that we tend to believe what we see, but every magician knows how easy it is to fool the eye and instill false belief. Most of us live our lives under the illusion that what we see is real, but what we see is the result of brain processing. We do not have any direct contact with what is outside us (whatever direct contact could possibly mean).

There are other common illusions to illustrate the point. A rainbow is a beautiful illusion that needs three elements: water drops, the sun, and an observer. When you are facing the rainbow the sun will always be at your back. A rainbow is part of a circular arc of light created when sunlight is redirected into your eye by nearly spherical water drops. The center of the rainbow's circle, your head, and the sun are in a straight line. (I once looked down upon a rainbow from an airplane. The rainbow was now a complete circle with the shadow of the airplane at the center.) What is the point here? The rainbow you see is your rainbow—no other person can see it! They may see a rainbow, but it will be their rainbow, with different water drops participating, and it will be in a different location. The center of their rainbow will be aligned with the sun and their head. Of course a rainbow can be photographed with a camera, so in that sense it does not depend on a brain. The illusion is the impression that we have of seeing a real arc of light, perhaps with a definite end. Were we to "chase the rainbow" to find that end we would encounter the illusory part of the phenomenon. You don't need to wait for rain to see a rainbow. Stand with the sun at your back and lawn sprinklers will make a rainbow but it will seem closer and not so spectacular. Even a single drop of dew on the grass can catch the sun and glow with color. As you move, the color changes.

A Clue from the Moon Illusion

Long ago Chinese artists discovered that when you shade a drawing of the moon with dark gradually fading to white, the moon will appear brighter (whiter) than the paper on which it is drawn.

Somehow the eye-brain system is designed to be sensitive to sharp discontinuities in shadow, color, pattern, etc., and it can get confused when the change is too gradual. As a graduate student, I had access to a red HeNe laser (one of the first). I cleaned up[37] its output (by passing it through a pinhole) and put its light on a distant screen where the "spot" was now about the size of a walnut. However, this "spot" had no definite edge or definite size. It was brightest at the center and gradually tapered off from there. The effect on my visual system was magnetic. I found my eyes jumping all around the "spot", looking for something they could not find...the edges. I captured the image on photographic paper and even the black-on-white image had that "where is the edge?" effect.

The image above doesn't do it justice, but you may get the idea of the illusion. We are best at seeing boundaries and breaks in patterns and can create distorted images of real-world situations that lack such features. What we see in these cases is the brain's best shot at interpreting the visual information.

Clues from Laser Speckle

The output of a laser can be cleaned up and expanded to make a spot of uniform brightness. Of course it is brightest in the center and slides smoothly to zero brightness toward the edge. But when it is viewed with unaided eyes–if you just look at the spot—there is a very evident speckle pattern, a graininess, seemingly covering the spot. Hold your head still and the speckles are still. Move or rotate your head, and the speckle pattern moves or rotates within the spot. The speckles seem to be out there covering the spot of laser light, but actually the speckling is an interference pattern formed on your retina.[38] No instrument would record any non-uniformity of laser energy off the spot itself. The spot is clean; the grains are you. On your retina, some rods and cones are being excited and others not. Your brain interprets this pattern as being "out there." Of course, this is our clue.

Not only the speckle pattern, but the screen, the floor, and the ceiling are, at the same time, light patterns on the retina. Just like the speckle pattern, all impressions of things being "out there," everything we see is a creation of the eye-brain system. WYSIRY.

Clues from the Color Illusion

Say you are a painter doing a still life of roses and a vase against a background. You blend some red and orange pigment and get the exact rose color. You even apply a daub to an actual petal and can't see any difference. You paint the rose, but when you add the background color, suddenly the rose color seems wrong. The background color affects your experience of the color used for the rose. Below is an example of this effect.

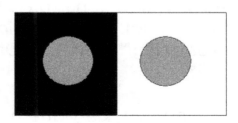

What we are viewing is two circles with identical gray values surrounded by different backgrounds. The two circles appear to be of different gray values. With color the effect is similar.[39] Of course all this points to brain processing behind our color vision.

There is a remarkable animated illusion that you can access on the web.[40] The background is a gray square with 12 small magenta circles placed like the numerals on a clock face. You are asked to focus on a mark at the center of the gray square while the spot at "1" turns off (goes to gray) for a tenth of a second. Then that spot returns to magenta and spot "2" turns off, etc. At first you are aware of the spots turning gray, but quickly it changes to the spot turning green (afterimage of magenta). For a while you see a green spot rotating around the "clock", but then that changes. The magenta spots, only one of which is off at any instant, all disappear, and you see only a single green spot circulating around. At first I couldn't believe this was an illusion—perhaps the animation was being manipulated to create these changes. So

I found my eyes constantly jumping from the center mark to the spots to verify they were still there and still magenta. You have to see this to believe it.

We have seen these classic illusions many times. We should pause and think about what these remarkable illusions have to teach us. The illusions are revealing something about our visual system. The images that reach our conscious awareness are highly processed by unconscious systems in our brain. These simple illusions reveal that the presentation is not always perfect. It is, after all, an internal display of a world external to us. These illusions are a reminder of what you see is really you...WYSIRY.

Clues from Moire Patterns[41]

The simplest Moire pattern can be seen by getting two hair combs and placing one atop the other. There will be places where the gaps (between the teeth) line up and you see through the combs; and places where teeth block your view. This creates the impression of dark and light bands superimposed on the teeth of the combs. These bands look a bit like a magnification of the comb's teeth. Just grab a couple combs and see for yourself.

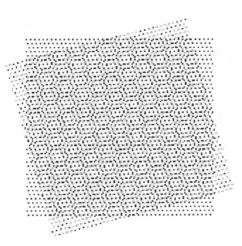

More interesting patterns are generated by screens—window screens work very well when one is placed over the other. If the screen has square holes, the moire pattern will look like giant squares, even when you are so far from the screen that you can't discern the tiny squares of either screen. If the two screen are not very flat, you will see a sort of wood-grain pattern of squares. If the screens have tiny circular holes, the moire will be of large circles.[42] When there is a gap between the two screens, which there usually is, then the pattern seen depends on the orientation of the two screens and the location of your eye. Since each of your eyes is in a different location, a slightly different pattern is seen with each eye. The brain interprets this as 3-D stereo information and represents the pattern as floating in space. Depending on screen-hole size, screen separation, and distance to the viewer, the pattern may appear to be in front, between, or in back of the screens. Moving the head moves the moire pattern, sometimes seeming to multiply the speed of the head movement. The whole pattern is generated by the brain, in the brain.

Years ago I saw a memorable moire at an artist/scientist exhibit.[43] Three wall-sized screens were suspended in a great hall. The moire pattern, also wall-sized, hovered in space, seemingly not attached to any screen. As I approached, the pattern appeared to zoom in from all sides to some minimum and then grow larger again as I approached. This was interactive art, generated by the eye/brain system.

Clues from Holograms

I hope you have seen a hologram and marveled at how a flat film can produce a 3-D image. To make a hologram; take a high-resolution photographic plate and set up some objects (the scene) near the plate, then simultaneously illuminate the scene and the plate with laser light (all on a vibration-free platform). The light reflected off the scene and the direct laser light on the plate will interfere to produce microscopic patterns on the photographic plate...like fingerprints. When the plate is developed and illuminated by direct laser light (imitating the original illumination) the pattern on the plate will diffract the light into a replica of the scene.[44] For me, the most convincing hologram is the front projection type. Illuminated from the rear, the plate creates a scene in front of the plate, seeming to float in space.

In the 1960s I visited a Museum in Washington, D.C., where there were two large holograms. One was of a person, so clear (in monochromatic green light) that you could see the hairs on the arm; even the laser speckle pattern was reproduced. The other was a projection hologram of a model speedboat. It seemed to hover in midair, in front of the large holographic plate. I was quietly leaning against the wall, viewing the illusion, when a young couple entered the room. The man went to a corner exhibit and the woman approached the boat. She hesitated as she put out her hand, perhaps remembering the "don't touch" prohibition. She obviously expected to touch something, but her hand went through the image. It seemed to me she instantly became fearful. Not wanting to investigate the happening, she said to her companion "Let's get out of here." I suspect her sense of reality was shaken.

This is a very good clue. It shows us that not everything that looks solid is real and that the feeling of something being real is generated by the brain. In this case, the light diffracted toward your eye by the holographic plate is real. The infolded information the light carries about the scene is real, but the objects that unfold from the illumination are not real. Reality is a feeling. WYSIRY.

I say "reality is a feeling" to bring attention to the comfortable feeling that accompanies our image of reality. Usually our brainscape is populated by objects (images) that our brain has identified: tree, grass, bug, Sharon...along with the feeling that this is real...it's ok. But sometimes we get a strange feeling that things are not right, something is amiss. Perhaps a shape approaches that we cannot identify and we feel strange. The woman who tried to touch the hologram of a speedboat had her comfortable feeling of reality shaken when her hand passed through what she expected would produce the feeling of solidity (of reality). The feeling of reality is so ever-present that we only notice it by its absence.

Clues from Virtual Reality

Television screens have become larger and sharper but, entertaining as they are, only toddlers and pets treat their images as reality. We realize early on that the TV image is not the thing-in-itself. The illusion lacks depth, the 3-D quality, since each eye sees the same image. However, if two miniature TV screens with appropriate optics are mounted on a helmet worn by the observer, the 3-D effect is reproduced. Motion sensors can be included so turning one's head will produce a corresponding change in the TV presentation. The effect is reported to give the sense of reality...virtual reality. People say they feel present in a space occupied by objects "out there." Some experimenters add touch to the virtual reality by the use of gloves that press on the fingers to simulate contact with an object. Grasping a virtual object with your virtual hand will produce a sense of touching; moving your hand will move the virtual object. Thus, one not only observes the virtual world but interacts with it.[45]

The easiest way to get a virtual reality experience is to attend an IMAX 3-D film presentation. (You can find a theater in major cities.) To view the show, you must wear polarizing glasses (sometimes the glasses have stereo sound built into the ear piece). Special screens with glass beads reflect polarized light, enabling full-color images to be presented separately to each eye. The screen can be 40 feet wide and just as tall, engaging peripheral vision. Even though you may be 20 feet from the screen, the 3-D objects seem to be just in front of you. The sense of reality is so strong that I, and most of the audience, feel the need to touch the image and verify that nothing is really there. I remember one scene of people seated at a table in a café. Wearing the glasses, I felt I was there too; my hair "stood up." It was a spooky feeling.[46]

In such a presentation, we know it is a movie, we know it is not real, but we get absorbed in it. We can, momentarily, lose track of actual reality and enter into a virtual reality. The point is, again, that what we think is our actual reality is a virtual reality, with the experience not momentary but extending over our lifetime.

A Little Recap

We have been focused on clues from the visual sense to gather clues which support the contention that the world we see around us is in fact a phenomenal world. A world produced by and in our brain from data supplied by our senses.

A person in Plato's Cave is convinced the shadows are reality, but careful observation of the shadows could cause doubt to creep in. We are in the same position, as we (our brains) are in the cave of the skull and are convinced the images we see are reality. Careful observation of these images reveals inconsistencies that cause us to doubt that what we experience is what it seems to be.

Having more or less exhausted the visual clues that reveal what you see is really you, and before we move on to clues from the other senses, we can pause to imagine an updated conversation between Socrates and Glaucon. Glaucon has absorbed all of the visual clues we have examined, and his view has been altered.

Glaucon: I get it now! What a fool I was thinking that I knew it all...all that mattered anyway. Now my whole concept of myself living in a world I thought was real is shaken. You have helped me see that this world I once said was outside me is a virtual reality, an image of an external world, that is really taking place in my brain. It is me, so to speak.

Socrates: How could it be otherwise? We accept that the brain is the vital organ of perception and that its connection to the world outside is through the nerves. From nerve signals we make a picture of what is out there. What finally got through to you?

Glaucon: It was when I donned that virtual reality helmet. After being in it for only a few minutes, I began to feel I was in that alternate virtual reality generated by the computer. I felt I was in it just as I now feel I am in this reality. Both feelings are the same, but the reality-helmet world is obviously virtual, so why couldn't the world I call "real" be virtual too? It could be virtual, I thought. I could be staring at my own virtual reality. There seems to be no reason to claim it's not. There could be a reality outside of me, but surely what I experience is just my personal representation of it.

Socrates: I see you have the basic idea, but the full impact of the situation may not have hit you yet.

Glaucon: What do you mean?

Socrates: Contained in your virtual world, at its center, is a virtual image of your body. The virtual world changes, but the body image remains at the center. This leads to a remarkable illusion of a body viewing the scene. Let us come back to this point after we look a some more clues from the other senses.

chapter

TWO

"Art bids us touch and taste and hear and see the world, and shrinks from what Blake calls mathematic form, from every abstract form, from all that is of the brain only."
—William Butler Yeats, "The Cutting of an Agate"

"Touch is the most fundamental sense. A baby experiences it, all over, before he is born and long before he learns to use

sight, hearing, or taste, and no human ever ceases to need it. Keep your children short on pocket money but long on hugs."
—Robert Anson Heinlein

Clues from Touch

We have been focusing on visual clues to help appreciate the personal nature of our private conscious experience. We have other senses that can provide clues in addition to the optical ones to which we have been attending. Let us turn our attention to the sense of touch. Traditionally we are said to have five senses: sight, taste, smell, hearing, and touch. But we also have a proprioceptive sense (body position) and a sense of balance, both of which could be included in this discussion of touch.

Touch may be the most certain sense. 3-D illusions created by glasses or holograms are real enough to fool the eye, so people reach out to check the scene with touch. "Seeing is believing" is not as trustworthy as "getting the feel of it." Touch is less easily fooled...but there are a few good touch illusions. That is, playing with touch can provide us with clues for our endeavor.

The Shaving Illusion

Here is one I noticed while shaving some 40 years ago. My face is lathered and the razor is pulling on my skin, but I can't actually see my face or the razor except in the mirror. The feel of the razor on skin is synchronized with the mirror image of the razor on skin. I found, with a little practice, that it was possible to shift the feeling of razor on skin to the mirror image. The face in the mirror now coincided with the feeling of shaving. A touch illusion.

Think about this. In the brain, the optical system is physically separate from the touch system. The vision and touch signals go to different parts of the brain. The optic nerve signals go directly to the rear of the brain, while the touch signals pass up the spinal column to an area across the top of the brain. Toes and feet areas are near the mid-brain, hand and finger areas near the top, face and lip areas near the side of the brain. It is evident that being touched on the foot elicits a feeling different from being touched on the hand. These feelings are different from each other but are repeatable. Being touched on the foot gives the same feeling time after time. From these feelings we accumulate a kind of touch map of our body. We also have a visual map of our body. When we are young, the repeated experience of touching and seeing together—feeling a certain feeling and seeing something visually contact the foot—allows us to correctly associate the touch map and the visual map and label the feeling as being touched on the foot. The phrase "hand-eye coordination" refers to training one's muscles to perform some quick movement, and it coveys the notion of getting different brain areas to work together. With practice, we learn to coordinate our touch and visual senses.

However, we never see our face directly; only by use of a mirror do we have visual information about our face. In the shaving illusion, since there is no direct visual map of the face, we can learn to associate the feeling of shaving with the face in the mirror. I can watch the razor's image scrape on my face's image and transfer the feeling to where I see the action happening: in the mirror. This is a touch illusion and it points out how we construct our internal reality. Our brain generates a sense of what it feels like to be in our body—part of that sense is our touchmap.

The Phantom Hand

Even more remarkable than the shaving illusion is a touch illusion that requires a little preparation.[47] Sit at a table and place your left hand out of sight underneath it, say resting on a book that is on your knees. Place on the table, above the position of your left hand, a rubber glove stuffed with something to give a lifelike appearance (the more lifelike the better). As you watch, have a cohort stroke the fingers of the glove while simultaneously stroking the corresponding fingers of your hidden hand, using the same rhythm on both. Soon you will have the illusion that the glove is your hand, that is, the source of the feeling of being stroked.

In this case we really are being stroked on the hand, but our body map is not so accurate as to allow us to place the hand below the table. We have some sense of the angle of bending at each joint, but these sensations cannot locate the hand very precisely. When we see a rubber hand being stroked in unison with feelings of our hand being stroked, that is enough to have the brain associate the sight and the feeling...the feeling is now shifted to the rubber glove. The information from the visual system seems able to dominate the information from the touch system in this case as it also did in the shaving illusion. You might call this an out-of-hand experience.

With a more elaborate setup, this misplacement of the sense of your body can be even more exaggerated. You can experimentally induce an out-of-body experience.

Here I report that this illusory experience can be induced in healthy participants. In the experiment the participants wear head-mounted displays that are connected to two video cameras that are placed at some distance [about eight feet] behind the back of the participant. The experimenter then uses two rods to touch the person's actual chest, which is out-of-view, and the chest of the "virtual body" by moving one rod at a location just below the cameras. This elicits a vivid illusion that their "self," or center of awareness, is located outside their physical body, and that they look at their body from the perspective of another person ("out-of-body illusion").[48]

The quote above describes a person wearing a 3-D virtual reality helmet that is displaying the scene from the two video cameras. The subject sees a rear view of a body about eight feet in front of them. As in the rubber glove trick, the subject sees a body being touched while at the same time the experimenter is touching them. The visual system dominates, and the sense is that the touch is happening at the site vision indicates. The participant feels that he has left his body. His physical body is no longer at the center of his phenomenal world.

More could be said about the feeling of "being outside of the body" but the point here is that our brain collects information from our many senses and creates a 3-D image of the world that includes an image of the body. The hand we see in front of us is not the real hand, but an internal representation of it. Tricking eyes (with cameras and VR helmets) can trick the brain into incorrectly placing the image of the body in the brainscape. We live in this brainscape—it seems to be all around us, but is somehow a brain function.

Everything we see and feel is constructed by our brain, and these simple experiments can help us appreciate that.

Clues from the Pinocchio Effect

This effect[49] allows you to feel that your nose has become longer. You need two helpers. Sit with your eyes closed behind one helper while the other, behind you, directs your fingers to the nose of the person in front of you. The active helper uses your fingers to stroke or tap the person's nose while at the same time stroking or tapping your nose. In a few seconds you feel that it is your nose being touched by the fingers of your extended arm...you have a two-foot nose. Your body image has been manipulated to make you feel that your nose is very long.

In a related experiment,[50] you grasp your own nose with your fingers while your biceps muscle is stimulated by a mechanical vibrator. This reportedly creates the illusion that your arm is being extended, and since you are holding your nose, it feels as though your nose is growing longer. If your hand is placed on your waist while the biceps muscle is stimulated, the feeling is that of your waist changing size.

We don't have sensors to inform us of the size of our body parts, but we somehow unconsciously deduce the sizes from secondary clues. The image we create of our own body is apparently quite malleable.

Clues from Anorexia

It is now widely known that some people, mostly women, can have a condition whereby they view themselves as being fatter than they are. Even though they may actually be very thin, showing ribs and joints, when they see their reflection in a mirror they see fat. Their internal representation of themselves is not accurate. Their body map is wrong. The condition can lead to excessive dieting and ultimately be fatal. This provides a powerful clue to the power of our body image and how it can go wrong. The body image is a portrayal of what we think of ourselves.

Clues from Misplaced Pain

The touch system, which produces the touch map, can be confused when there are no visual clues to help locate the feeling, as when there is an internal injury causing pain. Tooth infections may initially be felt as pain in the temples or in the neck. Injuries to the lower back, perhaps irritating the nerves there, may give rise to the experience of pain in the foot or leg. Our brain creates a brainscape that includes a representation of our body. Sometimes errant nerves can misinform the brain with regard to tissue damage. We may feel pain in our foot and believe it to be injured, but we may be wrong.

Pain is not *in* the injured body tissue. Injury to tissue causes signals to be sent via the nerves to the brain. When these signals reach the brain, the brain generates the feeling of pain.

In certain situations the brain may put pain on hold. We have all heard of those cases where people are severely injured, but because it is necessary to get away from mortal danger they feel no pain until the urgency of the event has passed. Athletes often report getting injured in a game and yet do not feel the pain of the injury until later. The brain can override or suppress the feeling of pain when the circumstances dictate, and later when the time is right, allow pain to restrict movement and promote healing. All pain is in the brain (although the source may be signals from the body). I personally do not like pain and marvel at how some people train themselves to tolerate or even, so they say, eliminate it. Certainly they can pierce their flesh with needles or hang from hooks in their flesh. Pain is like color...created by the brain.

The effect of placebos on pain is well known, and gives evidence to the importance of thought/belief on the feeling of pain. If we think some pain medication will work, it may work just because we believe it will. (If all we want is relief from pain...what's wrong with that?) The effectiveness of placebos tends to fade with time, however.

The brain's pain system uses bodily chemicals, endorphin and the like, to control pain. Some chemical—opiates—are similar in structure to the body's endorphins and can also reduce pain...and promote pleasure. These opiates can have extremely powerful effects on the brain and lead to addictive behavior. The connection of chemicals and the mind is a strong clue as to the brain being the seat of conscious experience.

Strangely, the brain itself has no pain receptors in it. The actual brain tissue has no capacity to feel pain or touch. Surgeons can cut into brain tissue while the patient is awake and cause no pain. (This is sometimes done when doctors need to know what brain function may be affected by surgical procedure, like tumor removal.) Sometimes we complain of having a headache, as though our brain were aching, but the brain cannot ache. Frequently, we are suffering from aching neck or scalp muscles and incorrectly representing the pain as being inside the head. Our brain processes make the pain, and this is our clue.

There are people whose brains are unable to create the experience of pain. At first this may seem a blessing, but these people do not live for long. Pain is a signal that there is something wrong...something to be attended to immediately. Without pain, these people are far more likely to injure themselves, and because they don't know they are injured the damage goes untreated. Pain serves a good purpose, and we are fortunate our brains have evolved the ability to create the experience of pain.

Clues from Empathy

I read of a case where woman felt her body was being touched when she watched some other person being touched.[51] When she was young she thought everyone had the same feelings. Experimenters measuring her brain response while she watched others being touched found activity in the same area that responded when she herself was touched. There are neurons in the brain, dubbed mirror neurons, that create in the observer of an action, an understanding of that action. We all have mirror neurons. Most of us are less responsive than this woman, although we might feel squeamish seeing another person get injured. It might be a good thing for society if all of us feet more strongly the pain of others. Empathy of this sort can help us get along with other people.

Clues from Phantom Limb

The classic example of body map confusion is the "phantom limb" phenomenon. Many people who lose limbs through accident or disease report sensations in the missing member—often pain but not always. Sometimes the missing limb feels cold or itchy or bent or twisted. The limb is gone, but the body map of the missing limb is still active. This is a touch illusion and a good clue as to how our brain constructs our sense of embodied self. There is more to learn from observing our body map but first we should finish discussing the topic of touch, as touch is an important part of how we create our body map.

V. S. Ramachandran has uncovered some fascinating facts while working with patients who experience phantom limbs.[52] Touch input from points on the surface of our skin is conveyed by nerves, then mapped to points on the surface of our brain—roughly to a band across the top of the brain. One oddity of this mapping is that the large area devoted to the fingers is adjacent to the area devoted to the face. Ramachandran found that patients who were missing a hand would report a feeling of being touched in their phantom fingers when touched on certain areas of the cheek. As Ramachandran puts it:

> When an arm is amputated, no signals are received by the part of the brain's cortex corresponding to the hand. It becomes hungry for sensory input and the sensory input from the facial skin now invades the adjacent vacated territory corresponding to the missing hand.

This is another illustration that what we feel about our body is a function of our brain. By "feel" I mean the feeling of having a finger, as opposed to the finger feeling the keyboard I am using. When the brain gets the feel of the body wrong, there can be problems like phantom limbs or anorexia.

Clues from Our Fingertips and Tongue

Try this touch demonstration[53] with your eyes closed: using the index and middle fingers, feel some bumpy surface, like the buttons on your shirt or a coin on the table. By sliding the finger pair around, you can get a fair impression of the surface configuration. Now perform the same procedure with the two fingers crossed. Each fingertip is getting the same information, but not in the usual order. We don't ordinarily touch or grasp objects with crossed fingers, so our brain is not good at uncrossing the information. It's a though our finger map remains crossed, and hence a good "picture" does not arise.

The other day I was unable to avoid doing a little plumbing job beneath the sink, where I could not see directly. Feeling around with my fingertips I began to form a "picture" of the situation. It seemed to be clearer when my eyes were closed. I discovered that a hex nut needed tightening, and I was able to guide an appropriate box wrench to the nut by touch. Our fingers are highly sensitive...a disproportionate amount of area in the touch region of the brain is devoted to the fingers (and also the tongue).

There are several different types of touch-sensitive cells in our skin: thermoreceptors to signal warm or cold, nociceptors to signal pain from skin deformation or intense temperature, cells to detect pressure, cells to detect drag or sliding motion (edge detectors), cells to sense vibration, cells to detect hair movement. These cells report to a part of the brain specialized for the spatial tactile sense called stereognosis. Touch helps us visualize the solid world in contact with us.

Our sense of touch adds solidity and texture to our image of the world around us. Surprisingly, we do not need to touch things directly to get this information. Even when wearing shoes and socks we create an impression of the character of the surface beneath our feet—soft, hard, rough, smooth, sandy, stony, etc.. Unsighted people can learn to extend their field of touch by means of a cane or wand. You can get a feel for this extension by closing your eyes and touching things around you with a chopstick or pencil. With only a little practice you can feel different textures and qualities in the objects you touch with your wand. Holding the wand, you get the feeling that this is where you end. Similarly, when we hold the wheel while driving we get the "feel of the road." As a passenger we are feeling with the "seat or our pants". We form an impression of the driving surface that is incorporated into our image of our environment. We can feel a slick road or a sandy surface and adjust accordingly.

Paul Bach-y-rita has developed a prototype touch-based device that interfaces a video camera with the tongue.[54] A computer scans the video picture and converts it to 12 x 12 dot picture. This is connected to an array of dot-like metal electrodes, which stimulate the tongue with electric pulses. Subjects report that they soon lose awareness of the device on the tongue and perceive the pulses as shapes and features in space, like seeing very dim shadows. In some of his tests, blind subjects are able to intercept a ball rolled toward them. Unsighted people have been tested at 20/800 vision level, but of course this will improve as the number of dots increases. The tongue is very sensitive—just notice the impression it produces when you feel your teeth with it. Somehow, the brain can use this Braille-like data to generate images similar to those coming from the optic system. Used in this way, the tongue makes a visual impression not a taste fantasy. The brain seems to be hungry for data about the world outside. Sighted people are aware of how the eyes feed the brain to generate a 3-D representation of the world, but data from touch can do the same.

Teeth, because they are firmly embedded in the gums, have a sensitivity to touch. When you floss your teeth, pay attention to the floss as it finds the gaps between the teeth. Even though it is just string on tooth, an image of teeth and gap is generated. This is a subtle clue to our brain as generator of our body map.

It is interesting that touch—and all the senses really—responds mostly to change. With your eyes closed, place your finger tips on a textured surface, maybe your shirt, but hold them still. Not much is sensed. Slide your fingertips over the surface slowly and steadily, and the texture appears. To read Braille, you must slide your fingertips over the tiny bumps in the surface to be aware of their configuration. Merely touching an array of bumps without sliding will not reveal their message. It's the minute changes that are felt.[55]

Step into a hot bath and the water initially feels very hot, but it soon feels quite normal (at least until you get overheated). Enter a warm room or a cold one, and at first you are aware of the temperature, but soon you cease to notice it. It is the difference that enters our consciousness. Our consciousness seems designed to be sensitive to change, and constant stimuli quickly fade from consciousness.

It is similar with the sense of proprioception. Sensors in the muscles and tendons—

proprioceptors—report back to the brain the position and tension in various parts of the body. Even with our eyes closed, we know where our hands are, but not exactly. When we are fatigued or a little tipsy, we may have trouble touching a finger to our nose with the eyes closed. Even in normal condition, we may not be very good at the exercise. Our proprioceptors are more tuned to the tension and angles of joints than to the exact location of our limbs in space, though practice can improve proprioception.

The proprioceptive image can be dimmed if the body is held very still. With your eyes closed try lying on your back in a comfortable position that you can relax into without effort. Don't move. Be very still. After a while, proprioceptive signals diminish. Your conscious sense of body position fades. Where are your hands? You can even fade into a sort of "out-of-body" experience. With no change of body position, the body map fades and an unusual "no-body" feeling can arise. Of course breathing and heartbeat continue and cause minute changes that degrade the loss-of-body feeling. This exercise serves to illustrate how the sense of being embodied, in a body, is generated by changes in proprioceptive signals.

This topic of our body map deserves more attention, and I will return to it later. One of the most important distinctions presented in consciousness is that between self and other. It is obviously necessary to know what is you and what is not you. The images in our consciousness arrive tagged with that distinction. For example, I just "know" that cup "over there" is not part of me, but this knee image is part of me. Some people with damage to certain parts of the brain get confused as to self and not self. They may deny that their arm belongs to them. Their body maps are severely "out of touch" with reality.

It is clear that all the senses have the trait of adaptation in common. Going from a dimly lit room into bright sunlight initially seems almost painful, but in a short while the vision system adapts. You may recall that vision actually fades away if the saccadic movement of the eye is suppressed. With sound, we may fail to register the constant hum of the refrigerator. With taste, hot salsa may fade into mild. We may cease to notice the odor in a recently painted room. Entering an air-conditioned room, the initial coldness soon feels just right. These examples of sensory accommodation indicate that a constant input to our senses soon loses its impact. The input must change to be noticed in consciousness. Our consciousness is a dynamic process, consciousness requires change. When change ceases, consciousness ceases.

Clues from Temperature

There is not just one type of temperature sensor in our skin—there are actually two. Each is anatomically and physiologically distinct from the other. Briefly, one senses warmth and the other cold.[56] The sensations of warm and cool are also qualitatively different—the feeling of warmth is different from the feeling of coolness. Each is a feeling, generated by our brain to represent some important feature of the external world.

To demonstrate this point, there is a well-known temperature illusion, which you have probably encountered. One hand is placed in hot water while the other hand is placed in cold water. When both hands are placed in room-temperature water, the water feels cold to the "hot" hand and hot to the "cold" hand. An interesting variation on this experiment is to get two coins cold in the freezer and place them on a table with a room-temperature coin between them. Then place your middle finger on the center coin and the index and ring fingers on the cold coins. Amazingly, the middle finger feels equally cold.[57] If you have a cold drink at hand you can recreate another version of this touch illusion by touching your middle finger to some neutral thing (a finger of the opposite hand will do) and the two adjacent fingers to the cold glass. Again you will find that the middle finger report a cold sensation...all three fingers feel cold.

This is a touch illusion. What our touch system is reporting in these trials is not reality. All the senses contribute to our brain-scape. They create the show which we accept as real. The show seems real, but it is actually the brain's representation of the information received by the senses.

Clues from the Cutaneous Rabbit

The cutaneous rabbit is a cute name for the unexpected feeling that can occur when a subject's arm is tapped in a certain way. I have never experienced this phenomenon, and unless you know someone in a psychology lab you probably will also never have the opportunity. However, this experiment[58] is often cited in books since it gives clues about how we generate our sense of time. A person sits with an arm on a table and with mechanical tappers in contact with the arm. The person might be given three taps on the wrist (about a tenth of a second apart) followed by two taps on the elbow, and then two more taps on the upper arm. Rather than feeling the taps at the three places where they were applied, the subjects report a series of taps "hopping" up the arm. A person has no trouble feeling separate taps applied to the arm at the points mentioned above, but when the taps are executed in a certain rhythm, the feeling is of a tiny creature jumping along the arm. There are no taps in the middle of the forearm, only at wrist and elbow, but the brain creates the false sensation of taps in the middle.

What does this demonstration point out? You actually experience the false sensation. It is real to you. It is a genuine experience—not created by a rabbit, but created by your brain. This means your brain creates your experience. In this case, it creates the experience of being touched on your mid-forearm. It doesn't create this experience out of thin air; the sensation is not a hallucination, though of course some brains are capable of producing hallucinatory experiences. Your brain creates the touch of the rabbit out of the pattern of taps on your arm. Wouldn't it be interesting to find out how your brain does that? At this point it is still a mystery, but it points to the fact that there is much more going on than meets the eye when we simply feel a touch. We can no longer just take touch for granted. Great and fascinating mysteries are involved.

It is also interesting to see the similarity of this illusion to the visual one we discussed above where two flashes of light slightly separated in space seem to be one light moving between the two locations. Does this similarity point to something in common about how the brain generates the reality we experience?

chapter

THREE

"Is no one inspired by our present picture of the universe? Our poets do not write about it; our artists do not try to portray this remarkable thing. The value of science remains unsung by singers: you are reduced to hearing not a song or poem, but an evening lecture about it. This is not yet a scientific age."

—Richard Feynman

Clues from Hearing

Hearing, in some sense, can be considered an extension of the sense of touch. Have you ever watched a tiny insect moving about on your arm, but been unable to feel it because it is so light in weight? If it encounters some hairs and disturbs them, you might feel it. Hairs, like levers attached to skin cells, are exquisite touch amplifiers. (I once overheard teenagers amusing themselves with the notion of Hell being not fire or ice but perpetual plucking of nose hairs.) Minute hairs in the ear are the ultimate sensors of the vibrations in the air that are the source of sound. The hairs respond to the vibrations by sending signals along the auditory nerves, which, when reaching certain brain areas, produce the sensation of sound.

I am having a little trouble writing about sound. It is cumbersome to use the word "vibrations" when the word "sound" is more natural. I think we appreciate that vibrations are external and sound is internal. Knowing this, I will sometimes use the word "sound" rather than "vibration" because it reads better.

This chain of reasoning is encrypted in the time-honored question: If a tree falls in the forest and there is no one to hear it, does it make a sound? Of course the crashing tree generates vibrations in the air, but these vibrations are, by themselves, not sound. Sound is the brain's response to the nerve signals reaching it. A falling tree makes no sound...the brain makes sound. Sound is our extension of touch into the world around us.

The sound we create not only has properties of loudness, pitch, and timber, but, because we have two ears, we can attribute a direction to the incoming vibrations. Our first clue is the difference in intensity. Sounds coming from the right side will be louder in the right ear than in the left. But there is additional information in the minute difference in the time of arrival at the two ears.[59] Our ears have a shape that has directional sensitivity. We are relatively insensitive to vibrations coming from below, but if we don a wide hat while walking then suddenly we become aware of the vibrations from our feet as they are reflected by the brim. Mostly our ears are tuned to the front with less attention to above and below. We are not very tuned to pick up our own voice, but we can enhance our ears by cupping a hand around the ear and talking into the palm. I have seen actors doing this as they synchronize their voice to animation.

There is an amusing sound illusion that is not so hard to recreate. Insert a hose into each ear and position the open end of each hose near the opposite ear, sort of reversing the ears. Sounds on the right will now seem to be on the left. Making one hose longer than the other will introduce a time delay in the arriving vibrations which acts to shift the apparent direction of the sound. I have read that subjects wearing such reversing apparatus can quickly learn to compensate, and can locate sounds quite well after a learning period.

My point (again) is that vision, touch, and hearing information is collected by separate sensory systems, initially going to different areas of the brain. Visually you might see an object fall and strike the earth. Aurally you hear a thud. These are separate experiences, but repeated instances will train the brain to bind them together. The person, the brain, needs practice to put the information from these separate systems together. Reversing the ears with the hose trick will throw you off for a while, but you can learn to correct the experience. What you see—and hear—is really you, but you have had to learn how to put it all together.

Clues from Bats and Other Creatures

In a much mentioned article,[60] Thomas Nagel asks: What is it like to be a bat? Bats emit repeated bursts of high-frequency vibrations and collect the echoes with their large ears. With this technique, the bat can locate and capture small insects on the wing in the dark of night. The insects are "illuminated" (insonorated?) by the clicks and chirps, and the bat, presumably, can make some kind of three dimensional representation of its environment. Perhaps differences in the quality of the sound reflection—say from smooth versus rough texture—result in color differences in the bat's phenomenal representation. We could possibly do tests on bats and determine if they indeed can detect texture. But, as Nagel points out, we will never really know what it is like to be a bat.

Some unsighted people have trained themselves to ride bicycles and navigate around obstacles by emitting repeated chirps and being attentive to the echoes. They get quite good at this and can distinguish brush-echoes from car-echoes and report getting a feeling of shapes out there arranged in space, similar to vision although much less detailed. Perhaps this human trick is similar to the capacity of bats. Nagel asks the question for more philosophical reasons, but we humans can at least appreciate the possibility that collecting vibrations can produce some kind of internal representation of what is out there.

Many creatures react to vibrations and perhaps they too have some kind of internal show going on. Water bugs respond to minute vibrations of the water surface as they stand on it (making use of the surface tension of water). Worms, intimately contacting the soil, seem to sense the slightest vibration of the earth. Whales communicate hundreds (perhaps thousands) of miles via vibrations (sounds) in the ocean. (People now question whether sonar devices confuse the whales.) Elephants are known to communicate via frequencies too low for us to detect with their ears. I find it easy to believe that they too have some kind of internal soundscape to inform them.[61]

Speaking of sounds of which we are usually not aware, consider this: There is, in our inner soundscape, an ever-present sound to which we have accommodated. It is always there, so we learn to ignore it. The sound can be described as a sort of quiet hiss, a gentle white noise. As a physicist, I would guess it is due to the action of air molecules impinging on the eardrum but a biologist might have a different explanation. Go into a very quiet place, and with a little practice you can learn to hear it. But the sound is present at all times—I can bring it to attention any time I choose. It is there for anyone to tune in to. There is an analogous background "noise" with vision. If you were to go into a completely dark room and cover your eyes with a dense pillow, you would not see uniform blackness. There is a difficult to describe, granular effect (phosphenes) in your brainscape, which some people describe as a "wall" in front of them.

The clue here is the usually unnoticed "noise" in our sound and vision systems that we can bring to attention. The "noise" is always there, and is a product of our representation process. This is a clue about "the show." We create the show. It is our private inner display of the world around us. The display is not completely clean—it contains a little noise, which we can learn to detect.

As humans we have become accustomed to the fact that many creatures have senses superior to ours. However, we can be proud of our auditory system–it can hold its own against any. Our vision, too, is excellent, but in the vision restricted forests and jungles from whence we came, hearing was an invaluable asset to survival. Our ears can detect the minutest of vibrations. However, the tiny hairs, that do the job are vulnerable to strong vibrations. They can be permanently injured by high-decibel "sounds." Many musicians now wear earplugs to prevent this type of damage, typically loss of hearing in the high-frequency range. People of advanced age suffer similar hearing loss.

Our hearing, when we are young and fresh, has a range of about 20 to 20,000 vibrations per second. We simply do not hear vibrations greater than 20,000 vibrations per second but dogs and bats (and of course many other creatures) do. The pitch of a flute or whistle depends on its length, so dog whistles are about an inch long and produce a vibration that dogs can hear but humans cannot. Bat chirps are about

40,000 vib/sec and thus could be sensitive to echo details of fractions of an inch.

On the low end of the spectrum, elephants can produce subsonic sounds around 10 vibrations per second. We can't hear those vibrations, but elephants can. Because of the long wavelength of these vibrations, the elephants probably use them for communication, not to form images. Earthquakes and tornados also produce low-frequency vibrations and perhaps that is why people report unusual animal behavior before the occurrence of such natural events.

We use high-frequency vibration, ultra-sound, to reflect off a fetus and make an image of it, but we cannot hear those vibrations. In a similar way, with similar equipment, we can detect reflected low-frequency vibrations, generated in a localized earthquake, to create a picture of the interior of the Earth. We can't hear those vibrations either. We have a limited ability to detect vibrations. When vibrations are in a certain limited range, we can detect their presence and use the information they contain to create an internal sound scene that is represented in our brainscape. The various sounds are the "paint" of a picture of the vibrational world outside us. The sounds have a direction, coming from the left or right, and they seem to be close or far in our recreation of the external world. The point here is that the reality is pressure vibrations in the air around us, and we interact with those vibrations to create the sounds that fill our brainscape.

An easily accessible sound illusion can be created when we use earphones. By controlling the relative volume to the left and right ears, sound can be heard to move from left to right, or it can seem to be in the center of your head. There is a kind of sound space, a soundscape created by the earphones, in which the various instruments of an orchestra seem to have different locations in space. This of course is a sound illusion, since the reality is synchronized vibrations entering each ear, followed by sophisticated brain processing.

Another interesting aspect of sound perception is how different it can be for different people. I had almost no music in my life as child, and later when I tried to make up for that omission by learning to play an instrument I found that if two notes were sounded together I couldn't tell which was higher. On the other end of the sound sensitivity spectrum are those people with perfect pitch, who can name any note upon hearing it. Tone-deaf, perfect-pitch, two vastly different worlds of sound. It's a clue that what we hear is not the same soundscape that others hear. Our brains, by birth and by experience, produce the sound experience we have. Sound is not in the world, it is in us. The world has its vibrations, but we are the sound.

Clues from the Deaf

One success of modern technology is the development of cochlear implants to provide some degree of hearing for deaf people. When loss of hearing is due to problems of the inner ear, some patients get partial restoration of hearing by surgically implanting a sound detecting device with electrodes inserted into the auditory nerve. The device imitates (somewhat) the signals generated by the hair cells in the cochlea by initiating pulses at a frequency of 1000 per second along multiple electrodes. The brain can actually interpret the signals as sound. The input is electrical but the experience is sound. The patients hear. This is a case where a malfunctioning bodily organ, the is replaced by an electronic component performing the same function. It converts air pressure vibrations into electrical nerve signals. This is something that most of us will not experience for ourselves, although we can appreciate the implication. When a person with a cochlear implant hears a sound, the sound is not out there in the world. Their brain is receiving electrical signals, coded with vibration information, from which the brain creates the internal sensation of sound. The point is that people with working ears do the same thing. We collect vibration information and create an internal soundscape. The vibrations are out there, but the sound is in here spread throughout our brainscape.

Clues from Sight/Sound Synchronization

In looking for clues to the manufactured and illusory nature of our phenomenal experience, we find two good ones involving the pairing of sight and sound. It takes sound (vibrations of course) 1/1000 of a second (1 ms) to travel one foot and thus about 20 ms to cross a room. When someone across the room is talking, their lip movements and the perceived sound are 20 ms out of synchronization. We don't notice this, because we assume the sight and sound should be in sync, and thus see it that way. When distances are much longer, we can't ignore the different arrival times of sight and sound.

Lightning strikes a mile away, and you hear the thunder five seconds later. Sitting in left field, you see the batter swing, but hear the crack of the bat half a second later. You hear an airplane overhead, turn to look in the direction of the sound, but see the plane well in advance of its sound. Fireworks explode and the bang follows.

We think we are sensing the world in real time as it is now, but that is not the case. Sound is slow and easily reveals the lie in the idea of immediate hearing. Light moves so fast that we must be quite clever to reveal the deception of immediate vision. Say (wearing dark glasses) you point directly at the sun. The sun is not actually in the direction you are pointing. The light from the sun takes about eight minutes to reach us, and in that time, the sun moves four solar diameters. It is two degrees off of where we are pointing. To point directly at the sun, you would have to more your finger westward by four solar diameters.

This delay is even more exaggerated for the stars. The light from all those stars we see with our unaided eyes has taken many years to arrive and thus the stars have moved very far from where we now see them. The star Rigel at the foot of Orion is 900 light-years away. The Andromeda galaxy, which you can see without a telescope if you know where to look, is 2,000,000 years back in time as you view it. The illusion that we are seeing things as they are now is very far off the mark when we view the heavens. Our mistake in thinking we hear sound immediately is made evident after a few dozen feet. Our phenomenal "now" consists of images of objects that have existed over an enormous span of time. Careful observations make this evident.

Clues from the Inner Ear

The sense of hearing is intimately connected to the sense of balance. Both sensory systems are physically connected to a small chamber of the inner ear, the vestibule, positioned after the eardrum and the tiny bones of the middle ear. The sense of balance is achieved by tiny hairs (very much like those responsible for hearing) that respond to the sloshing movement of fluid in canals connected to the vestibule.[62] This vestibular system informs us of changes in our head position, rotations left or right, and linear shifts—up/down, left/right, forward/back. Rotate or nod your head and you can still read this text. There is a rapid reflex signal that goes from the vestibular system to the brain, which produces eye movement opposite to the head movement, thus stabilizing our vision.

You can get a sense for this stabilization, if you have the stomach for it, by rotating yourself in a suitable chair or while standing. When you begin rotating, the fluid in the canals stimulates the hairs and you get the feeling of spinning but if you keep up a uniform spin rate the fluid calms down and the spinning feeling also calms down. When you stop abruptly, the fluid continues and you get the feeling of spinning in the opposite direction. Your feeling of spinning, or of being stable, is generated by the brain. The usual comfortable feeling of being stable in a stable world is a brain function. But it can be disturbed by illness, injury, disease, or by spinning yourself as just described. The condition known as vertigo causes people to feel they are spinning or out of balance. Excessive alcohol intake can induce the same effect. Our normal feeling of being in balance is produced by our brain, but a very unpleasant feeling can be induced by vestibular problems.

Astronauts, while in orbit around the earth, are in a condition of "free-fall" equivalent to being in a situation with no gravity. Objects released by the astronauts don't fall, they just float (orbit) where they are released. In such conditions it is common for an astronaut, having lost a sense of up and down, to become disoriented. I've read that a sharp rap on the foot can restore the astronaut's equilibrium.

Many people are prone to motion sickness when riding in a car or on a boat. My mother avoided rocking chairs. The dissonance between the visual system, the vestibular system, and even the feeling of sloshing stomach contents can induce nausea. Most people, however, can adjust to these disparate inputs and gain their "sea legs". Perhaps the sense of balance should be added to the ordinary five senses. The sense of stability and balance is certainly ever-present in our brainscape, although we usually only notice it by its absence. The point being made here is that the feeling we ordinarily have of being stable and balanced is just that—a feeling. A feeling generated by our brain.

chapter

FOUR

"One cannot describe the taste of red pepper."
—Zen saying

Clues from the Tongue

Our tongues are not very good at generating tastes. Most of what we regard as taste, say that of an apple, is actually smell. When we have a blocked nose due to a cold, food is said to lose its taste. If you hold your nose closed, a piece of apple is hard to distinguish from a piece of onion. The texture of the two is different and gives it away.

The tongue is a chemical detector, but it must come in intimate contact with a substance in order to taste it. Dry sugar grains on a dry tongue elicit no taste, but on a moist tongue the characteristic sweetness is detected. The sugar crystals must dissolve in order to contact certain cells and trigger a response. It is described somewhat like a key operating a lock: only a certain shape of key will work the lock. Brass key or steel doesn't matter if the shape is right. Artificial sweeteners will taste sweet if they imitate the shape of sugar molecules. The clue here is that the sweetness is not in the sugar. It is our brain's response to the signals it gets from those certain cells. We produce the sensation of sweetness; it is not present in sweet things.

Though it is a bit off the subject, there is another interesting fact about sugar. Natural sugars, like fructose derived from fruit, are composed of fairly simple molecules that have a handedness. Your right hand and left hand are similar, though you can tell one from the other in a photograph. But a photo of your right hand viewed in a mirror looks like your left hand. Natural fructose is right-handed, in a laboratory you can make left handed fructose (which nature does not make). The left-handed variety has the same atoms as right-handed fructose, so in some chemical sense it is the same—it has the same formula. But the left-handed sugar does not taste sweet! The key does not fit the lock. The chain of events leading to sweetness is not initiated. We do not experience it as sweet. Incidentally, the body can't use it to produce energy either.

Traditionally we say the tongue responds with only a few taste sensations: sweet, bitter, sour, salty, and recently some researchers suggest there is another that they have named umami (savory).[63] All of these flavors are brain responses and can be shown to vary from person to person. Two foods stand out in the list of variable subjective taste—broccoli and cilantro. Some people enjoy the taste of these vegetables, while others find them bitter or objectionable. George Bush (the first one) was questioned as to why he didn't eat his broccoli at some lunch, and he replied "I'm the president of the United States of America, and I don't have to eat my broccoli if I don't want to."[64]

All tongues are not equal. Color blindness in a person is obvious when their socks don't match, but flavor blindness is much more difficult to detect. A clear case is that of the taste of phenylthiocarbamide (PTC), which tastes bitter to most people but is tasteless to others. Other such different tasting chemicals have been discovered.[65] Here is a clue that flavor does not reside in the substance but is in us, produced by our tongue-brain system. It is we who are bitter, sweet, sour, salty, and umami. The outside world is the stimulus for our internal flavor representations.

Another clue to the subjectivity of taste is that other animals have a different palate. Cats apparently do not experience the sweet taste we get from sugars, which correlates with their indifference to treats we humans delight in.

chapter

FIVE

"A rose by any other name would smell as sweet."
—William Shakespeare

"But when from a long distant past nothing subsists, after the people are dead, after the things are broken and scattered, taste and smell alone...remain poised."
—Marcel Proust

166

"And as soon as I had recognized the taste of the piece of Madeleine dipped in lime-blossom tea that my aunt used to give me (though I did not yet know and had to put off to much later discovering why this memory made me so happy), immediately the old gray house on the street, where her bedroom was, came like a stage to attach itself to the little wing opening onto the garden that had been built for my parents behind it."

—Marcel Proust

Clues from Smell

Our sense of smell is the last of our senses to which we can look for clues revealing our condition as inhabitants of the cave of the skull. The brain is our home, but it has no magical connection to the world outside of it and must create a representation of that world from information provided by the senses. Vision, our dominant sense, has provided a wealth of clues, along with many strong clues from touch. Hearing has contributed a few clues. Taste has not been very useful in our sleuthing, and smell will not be a great help either. Compared to other sentient beings, our vision, hearing, and touch get high marks, but taste and smell seem to be delinquent. Dogs have huge noses with elaborate nasal folds and put us to shame as smellers. It is obvious to anyone who has lived with a dog that they must have a very rich internal world of smell that we can only imagine. (However, we are far better than birds, which have little sense of smell.) Perhaps our tongues and noses have lost the sensitivity they once had. In our civilized lives, taste and smell may not be as important to survival as the other senses, but they certainly make a huge contribution to our quality of life. People who have lost their sense of smell, anosmics, often suffer from depression and a reduced quality of life.

It is said that smell is the sense most strongly tied to memory. One reason for saying this is because of our knowledge of brain anatomy. At the bottom of each brain hemisphere is an elongation (olfactory bulb) that protrudes toward each nasal cavity. Nerve axons from these two brain extensions extend cilia through the bone into the nasal cavity. The bulbs connect to older parts of the brain closely associated with forming memories.[66] Certainly odors can evoke thoughts of events long passed and otherwise unremembered. The other day a passing scent of burning leaves reminded me of childhood memories of huge piles of leaves, smoldering, crackling, and smoking. Where I live now we can't burn leaves, and I miss that autumnal perfume.

The cilia, immersed in mucus, can detect upwards of 10,000 odorants that must be capable of dissolving in the moist film that coats the interior of the nose.[67] Some people categorize these odor sensations as fruity, flowery, resinous, spicy, foul, and burned...somewhat like the categories of taste. One clue we get from the nose is the wide range of sensitivity among people. Some people smell badly (which is better than stinking badly), while others can discriminate subtle differences in wines and perfumes. Another clue from the nose is the different response people have to certain odorants. The chemical amylacetate gives a banana experience to most people, but is odorless to a small fraction of people. There are other examples of differently perceived odorants and they point to genetic differences in our individual abilities to create our smellscape.

All of us do not have the same odor landscape. We differ greatly in that respect. This should be a clue that odor is not in the external world. We each create odor in our internal world according to our varying abilities.

In a recent article in *Nature*[68] you can read of an investigation of smell using fMRI brain scans to locate two areas of the brain associated with smell. One area is active when sniffing in through the nose—orthonasal olfaction—and the other is active when air exits out through the nose during mastication or swallowing—retronasal olfaction. The retronasal odors, detected in the nose during chewing, are referred to the mouth and are experienced as if they were within the mouth. These odors are called "flavor" and are a large part of what we call "taste." The point for us is that the brain causes us to experience the odors not in the nose but in a different place, the mouth. This is the correct thing to do of course, but notice that this is not done when sniffing in during orthonasal olfaction. This is a very subtle clue, in which our brain uses olfactory information to create an experience of taste in the mouth.

Another clue: if you have ever had a migraine or severe headache, your odor landscape can change its contours. Ordinarily pleasant odors can become disgusting. Every odor becomes unpleasant, somehow distorted by what ever is happening in the brain at the time of the headache.

Another subtle clue is the emotional reaction we have to odors. Our cultures condition us to accept or reject certain odors. Many city dwellers find the odor of horse manure disgusting but farmers or gardeners can come to appreciate its qualities. My mother always winced at the taste of wine or beer, but other people warp their lives around those tastes (which are actually odors). I have tried unsuccessfully to enjoy the taste of kimchee (fermented cabbage), but most Koreans love it. Odor detection is one thing, but our reaction to those odors is another. We are trained by our culture to like certain odors and reject or ignore others. Just think of how various cultures react to the odor of human feces. Odor is a (conditioned) response to external odorants. Odor is not out there but in here, created by our brain.

Clues from Pheromones

Pheromones are biological chemicals released by one member of a species to communicate something to another member. Moths emit a sex-attracting hormone and ants lay down trail-marking chemicals. Dogs use chemicals to mark territory. Other living things signal alarm or aggression with pheromones. But the situation with humans is far from clear.[69] Men make a biochemical called androstadienone, which is said to be attractive to women. Women in turn produce estratetraenol to attract men. However, it has been difficult to document the effectiveness of these pheromones, which by themselves are odorless. Their effect, if any, is on a subconscious level. When meeting a potential partner, people often say "the chemistry was good" meaning they enjoyed the contact. Perhaps this is a subtle recognition of the pheromones at work. Also some researchers suggest that pheromone signals may communicate the compatibility of immune systems. Others suggest that sexual orientation may be guided by pheromones. One study found that the response of women to male pheromones correlated with the ups and downs of their monthly cycle. At the time they were most fertile they were most likely to rate the male odor as attractive. Their sense of smell was not constant; it varied with their period. We can deduce that the experience of smell can vary with body chemistry which points to smell being "in here" rather than "out there."

Less controversial is the evidence that when women live together, as in a dormitory, they tend to synchronize their menstrual cycles. The women may have had different cycles before they came together but in time they tend to get in step.

Is there a clue in all this? Perhaps. Besides the senses of sight, touch, hearing (and proprioception and balance), taste and smell, perhaps we get information via pheromones. The pheromones may have a subtle effect on the brainscape in that they may influence our feeling about someone we meet beyond how they look and sound. This is not indisputable, but we are looking for every clue we can find.

Clues from Synesthesia

"Riding in a car, I was about 11, and I said, 'The number 5 is yellow.' My father said, '5 is yellow-ochre.' My mother and brother looked perplexed."
—Carol, a synesthesiac

Synesthesia is when one sensory input produces two or more sensory effects in a person's conscious experience. We see in the quote above that Carol was 11 years old before she became aware that not everyone sees numerals in distinct colors. She would see colors when others would see black and white. For her the printed numeral 5 would appear to be colored yellow. Other numerals would have different colors. The correlation is constant and involuntary. Every day, 5 is yellow and the impression is that it is real, out there, not happening in the head. Other synesthesiacs, like Carol's father, might have a different color palette associated with the numerals, but the palette is constant for each individual.

Many people have reported similar pairings of senses, although most involve color: musical tones have color, letters of the alphabet have color, text has color, words have color, tastes have color, pain has color. But other combinations have been reported: music evokes shape, touch (say acupuncture) evokes color and shape, smells evoke shape and texture, odors evoke taste (road tar odor is salty). And more complex combinations: numbers and letters evoke color, gender, or personality.

Synesthesiacs report a learning process, where first they think everyone experiences the world as they do, and then they discover they are different. Herein is our clue. We all think at first that everyone is seeing the world as we do. We all think at first that we see the world directly, as it actually is, so of course others must be seeing the same world in the same way. Perhaps people with synesthesia are fortunate, not only because they have a richer sensory experience, but because they can discover WYSIRY at an earlier age.

While researching synesthesia, my first experience with acupuncture came to mind. A needle was placed near where my thumb and forefinger meet, and then the needle was slowly rotated by the practitioner. This evoked in me a confusing impression of a huge log, like a telephone pole, rotating end over end. Perhaps all of us in certain circumstances can experience the mixing of the senses. In fact as many as one in a hundred people may have this experience. You may be one of these people, and this is a clue for you—-a clue that you are seeing the shadow on the wall of your cave.

Clues from Missing Senses

There are many senses that we humans lack but that other living things possess. The relative weakness of our sense of smell compared to dogs is well known, but other animals have even more remarkable abilities.

Our color vision extends from red to orange, yellow, green, blue, indigo, and violet (ROYGBIV). To be more accurate, I should say our vision responds to only a narrow slice of the possible frequencies of electromagnetic field oscillations. Frequencies slightly higher than those we see as violet are called ultraviolet, UV. Certain birds and insects, bees for instance, respond to UV radiation, while we are visually unresponsive to it. There are some flowers, white to us, which are patterned in UV reflection, presumably to be attractive to their pollinators. Most mammals have only two color receptors in their retinas, we humans have three and birds top us with their four receptors.[70] The bird's fourth receptor is maximally sensitive in the ultraviolet. We can presume that they have a more colorful brainscape than we have. Just looking at the bright colors in their plumage, we can expect them to have excellent color perception. We are detecting UV when our skin tans or burns or when we get "snow blindness", but UV does not produce any effect in our consciousness (blindness, red skin, and pain aside).

On the other end of the spectrum, frequencies below those perceived as red are referred to as infrared, IR. If you put an iron poker in the fire when you pull it out it will glow "red hot," emitting a range of EM frequencies peaking in the red. As it cools and becomes visually dim it continues to emit EM energy at lower frequencies—infra-red radiation. All warm things emit infrared radiation. We can't see this radiation at all, but rattlesnakes can, and they use it to locate their warm, infrared emitting, prey in the dark. We humans have created IR detecting instruments, night vision glasses for example, but our eyes are blind to it. IR has no direct input to our consciousness. If we were sensitive to IR we could see people and animals in the dead of night, like in those police chase scenes we sometimes see on TV. Seeing IR or UV would seem to be possible but it is an ability we lack. We could have evolved to see these energies but we don't see them. And that is the clue from missing senses. Our conscious experience of the outside world is incomplete.

Some sentient beings can see what we cannot (except through our instruments of course) and this is a strong clue that what we experience is a representation of information gathered by our senses and not some direct sensing of the external world. Some beings can detect things in ways we cannot, because they have senses that we do not have. We experience the world of our senses, not the world itself.

As to the possibility of seeing the other parts of the electromagnetic spectrum, like radio, TV, microwave, X-ray, and gamma rays, I don't know of any creatures that can detect these radiations. We humans do have devices sensitive to these frequencies, and can convert the information to "false color" images, which can be very revealing about what is out there. The heavens around us have been scanned in all the EM frequency ranges and have produced many beautiful (false color) images leading to important discoveries. Our natural senses are blind to all but a narrow slice of the EM spectrum, centered around the peak frequencies emitted by our yellow-hot sun. Instruments are a big help and reveal that there is more out there than meets the eye.

There is an exception to the statement that no creatures can detect electromagnetic frequencies other than IR, ROYGBIV and UV. When the frequency is zero we get the case of static electric or magnetic fields and apparently there are life forms that somehow detect these fields. This ability, electroreception, is present in some fish, sharks, and rays. The only mammal known to have it is the platypus. Sharks have hundreds of spots along their snouts leading to gel-filled canals which, at their end, have a single tiny hair similar to those of the lateral line of fish and those of the human ear.[71] This enables the shark to detect the minute electrical signals generated by other animals muscles; they can "hear" your heart beating.

The platypus swims under water with eyes closed, but with the aid of its duck-like bill it can feel around and can sense the presence of minute electric fields created by (or disturbed by) small edible things. Perhaps, with the aid of its bill, the platypus forms an image of the electric presence of its prey.[72]

Perhaps creatures with electroreceptive abilities can do something like bats or radar. Bats emit high-frequency sound and listen for its reflection. Radar devices emit electromagnetic pulses (with wavelengths only somewhat longer than the bat sound waves) and listen for their reflection. Certainly creatures could have evolved to emit EM radiation, detect its reflection, and make an internal picture—like a natural radar screen.

Similarly, there is magnetoception—the ability to detect the orientation of Earth's weak magnetic field—which guides the migration of certain animals. The Earth has a magnetic field, originating in its metallic core, penetrating the core, mantle, crust, and atmosphere, and extending into space. Some creatures (pigeons, loggerhead turtles, spiny lobsters, rainbow trout, salmon, dolphins) can sense this magnetic field and use it to navigate around their home territory. A pigeon's navigation can be messed up by attaching a small, permanent magnet to its neck. Even some tiny water creatures, bacteria, use magnetite crystals in their bodies to sense the Earth's magnetic field and determine which way is up (toward the light).[73]

So we come to understand that there are aspects of the world, electric and magnetic fields, to which some living things respond but that are not part of our perceptual landscape. Perhaps, say in electroreception, the animals may even be capable of forming some kind of internal image of the field. We have no way of affirming or denying the possibility. But no doubt such animals can respond to these fields while we cannot.

There is yet another missing sense. We humans detect electromagnetic energy with our eyes and vibrational energy with our ears. Fish do the same, but they have also evolved an additional sensing organ called the lateral line. The line is a band of darker scales associated with sensors called neuromasts. Running from the gills to the tail fin on both sides of their body, it enables them to detect pressure changes in the water (also low-frequency sounds). There is a similarity between the sensors of a fish's lateral line and the tiny hairs that line our cochlea. Some fish have lateral lines that are sensitive to minute electric fields. These lines enable the fish to sense predators and prey, and account also for their schooling behavior. So besides their eyes and ears, fish have a lateral line to provide an even richer information source for their survival. Covering a fish's lateral line with tape will cause it to be blind in this sense. The fish loses its schooling ability.

Here again is a clue for us. Some creatures sense the world in ways that we do not. The world of their experience is different from ours. The scene we see and take to be real would be a different brainscape if it included some of the senses these animals have. What would it be like to experience magnetic or electrical fields? How would our brainscape be different if we sensed polarized light?

Clues from Color Blindness

Another WYSIRY clue is color blindness. Most of us are trichromats—we have three types of color receptors (cones) in our retinas. Each of the receptors gives some response to any visible light (red, orange, yellow, green, blue, indigo, violet) that falls on it. However, each type of receptor has a maximum response in a different section of the color spectrum—long, medium, and short wavelengths. Often these are referred to as the red, green, and blue cones, RGB. (Actually the green cone peak is more like yellow-green and the red cone peaks near the yellow.) Due to genetic delinquencies, we humans can be missing one, two, or all three receptors (monochromats). Genetics can also conspire to add a fourth cone. I've read that if the mother is missing the long wave detector and the father lacks the medium, then it's possible for them to have a daughter who has a forth type of receptor, which peaks between the medium and long (a tetrachromat). Such a person would have color discrimination abilities better than us trichromats.

How is this a clue? Say you, with normal color vision, and a dichromat friend are viewing three colored cards. To you, two look the same and one looks slightly different, but to your friend they all look the same. One way to describe this situation is to say that one of the cards "really" is different and that your friend is partially blind. Any "normal" person can see that one of the cards is different. But then imagine that another friend who is a tetrachromat comes along, and sees differences in all three cards. From her point of view, you are blind to the color differences. In the first case you are better at seeing color, in the second you are worse.[74]

With a little thought, you may come to accept that what appears to be color "out there" is a result of a chain of events involving the eye's retina, the optic nerve, and various vision centers in the brain. The electrochemical signals along the optic nerve, repeated tiny voltage spikes, are certainly not colored. They do carry information from the "color" receptors, but these voltages are not colored. In fact, these voltages are not different from the voltages that carry sound or smell information. The voltages are directed to particular brain regions, where the magic of coloring occurs. The brain makes the color. The color is you.

Philosophers and children have surmised that perhaps we all see different colors but because we are consistent in our naming, there is no way to prove or disprove the conjecture. Color is a personal addition to our representation of the world. I've read the speculation that some painters, (some say Mattise), might have an idiosyncratic color sense, which guides them in their choice of color palette. We people with normal color vision can take pride in our marvelous ability to color the world. Imagine a world of people who could see only in black and white. Your color vision would seem to them a miracle (which it is). There are patients who have suffered damage to the part of the brain that colors the visual scene; they report seeing only shadows of gray, and they find this very disturbing. Pity the monochromats.

We are all monochromats when the ambient light is dim. It takes a certain brightness to excite the color cones of the retina, so in the dimness of night only our color-insensitive retinal rods are working. We lose color and see in black and white. All cats are black at night. There is an interesting illusion involving the rods. Our rods can't detect colors, but they are better than the color cones at detecting weak light. When the light is dim there is a sort of hole in the center of our vision where the densely packed cones are concentrated (in the fovea). We see shapes and shadows in our peripheral vision but nothing in the center. In the autumn sky near Orion is a small group of stars called the Pleiades or the Seven Sisters, which attracts your attention in the corner of your eye as a bright glowing area. When you shift to look right at it, using your cones now, it loses its glow. Looking away, it brightens again. This is a subtle clue to WYSIRY.

Daniel Dennett, on page 31 of his book *Breaking the Spell* writes:

> One of the surprising discoveries of modern psychology is how easy it is to be ignorant of your own igno-rance. You are normally oblivious of your own blind spot, and people are typically amazed to discover that we don't see colors in our peripheral vi-sion. It *seems* as if we do, but we don't, as you can prove to yourself by wig-gling colored cards at the edge of your vision—you'll see motion just fine but not be able to identify the color of the moving thing. It takes special pro-voking like that to get the *absence* of information to reveal itself to us.

When I read this I was so amazed I could not accept it. I tried it myself with a deck of playing cards. I stared straight ahead and gradually moved cards, one at a time, into my peripheral vision. I was 100 percent accurate in judging their color. I asked a friend to try and the result was the same. I repeated it with my wife and other friends and invariably they too were 100 percent accurate. I did an internet search on "peripheral color vision" and quickly found several sites with data to show that peripheral color vision not only *seems* to be there but can be measured. One of them is:

http://www.alma.edu/departments/psychology/SP98/ZaMa/pcv.html).

So I find myself in a bind. Dennett is a major player in the field of consciousness. He regards this as an important clue. Has he actually tried it himself? I leave it to the reader to try the simple experiment and see what results. Perhaps it is a huge clue, but it is not one I can confirm.

A Clue from the Missing Sense of Gravity

Physicists need only invoke three forces to give a good explanation of the workings of matter: the nuclear force, the electromagnetic force, and the gravitational force.[75] The nuclear force, by far the strongest, holds protons and neutrons together in various combinations to create the nuclei of atoms. The nuclear force, although strong, is vanishingly small outside the nucleus. The electromagnetic force binds electrons to the nucleus and accounts for the various elements and provides the force to combine the elements into molecules and larger conglomerations (DNA, bodies, and brains). Gravity is the weakest of the three forces. However, it is always additive, unlike the plus and minus charges of the electrical realm. And the pull of mass is far-ranging, becoming vanishingly small only at infinity. Gravity holds our planet together, keeps us from flying off into space, and enables the earth to orbit the energy-giving Sun.

Of these three forces, the electromagnetic force is the only one we sense directly,

more or less. Our eyes are sensitive to electromagnetic waves in a very narrow band
of the possible waves. When these waves
terminate on the retina we experience the
familiar colors of the rainbow. The electromagnetic force thus connects directly to
the eye-brain system. Arguably all the senses utilize the electromagnetic force to work
their magic. They all connect to the brain
via nerves, which pass electro-chemical
signals. The receptors of the ear, tongue,
nose, skin, etc. utilize electromagnetic
properties such as elasticity and chemical
affinity, which are electrical in nature, to do
their work. Certainly our senses do not use
gravitational or nuclear forces.

Does our vestibular system of balance
sense gravity? Not really. Our inner ear, in
a system separate from hearing, has three
mutually perpendicular canals filled with
fluid (endolymph) and lined with sensitive
hairs. Gravity pulls on the fluid and its position is sensed by the hairs (not unlike the
hairs of the ear, which respond to air motion). So we don't directly sense gravity but
rather sense fluid movements via our ves-

tibular hairs, which operate electromagnetically.

So in some sense, we are missing a sense—the sense of gravity. We can look up and see the moon because we can detect the electromagnetic energy reflected off its surface, but if we had gravity sensors, we could feel the moons's massive presence. The moon's gravitational pull is weak, but it does cause the global tides of the oceans. Imagine if we could sense directly, as we do with electromagnetic radiation, the approach of a large mass (mass is inseparable from gravity). We could feel the presence of a car or person by the distortion caused in the surrounding gravitational field, without the need for detecting reflected light or sound. Such a sense might be very useful. It's a missing sense. The gravity forces are out there but we cannot detect them. (Nor, as far as we know, can any other creature.)

This is a clue because we know through our instruments that the world contains forces that we cannot sense. What we do sense we incorporate into our representation of the world, but the direct sense of mass (through gravity) is lacking.

chapter

SIX

Clues from Our Sense of Time

The time dimension is not as visual as the spatial dimension. Of course we have all had the experience of time seeming to pass slowly (when we are bored) or quickly (when we are occupied), but there is a more profound aspect to our time sense.

In the 1960s, Benjamin Libet did some important tests on patients who had their brains exposed for surgery. He stimulated localized points of the brain surface with a mild pulsed electric current. The subjects, who had to be awake for the surgery, would report sensations on their skin, warm or cold feelings, or sometimes more specific sensations such as water drops on their skin. Libet noticed that it took about half a second of stimulation until the patient felt anything. Libet was observing that the conscious experience is half a second late—the feeling of immediacy is an illusion.[76]

One of the characteristics of conscious experience that often goes unnoticed until it is mentioned, is the feeling that it is happening right now. We feel we experience things instantaneously, without any delay. Sure, we know that nerves take time to transmit their signals to the brain, yet somehow we feel that we see it all happening in the moment, right in front of us. But that is not the case.

Our sense of what is happening now cannot be extricated from our memory of what has happened in the past and our anticipation of what the future will bring. No one has done a better job of writing about a single moment of consciousness than John McCrone. In the following quote he is considering tennis and cricket players.

Each player began with broad expectations, usually dictated by their knowledge of the capabilities of their opponents or thoughts about what their opponents might need to achieve due to the state of the game. Then, watching their opponents shape up would start to give them general hints about how to prepare—perhaps enough for a cricketer to decide whether to step on to the front or back foot, or a tennis player to begin swivelling left or right. But the guessing games never stopped. Tests showed that the first 100 milliseconds, then the second 100 milliseconds of the ball's flight would lead to a steadily more accurate idea of what to expect. The skilled players were refining their state of expectancy right until about 200 milliseconds before contact, by which time, as McLeod's experiment showed, the brain could no longer physically react. If something happened to a ball that late even the most accomplished player would swing and miss.

Our large brains are necessary to help us when things are changing rapidly, whether we are hitting tennis balls or swinging through the trees. A tennis ball can move 20 feet in 200 milliseconds but the information that informs our experience of now is 200—300 milliseconds old (due to the time is takes for signals to pass along our nerves). Our conscious display is a calculated display of what things should look like (feel like) in the now, based on what was sensed in the past. The tennis ball we see in our brainscape is not the actual tennis ball but an anticipated tennis ball. If things go right, the actual ball is where we judge it will be, and we strike it with the racquet. I got a sense of this when I cranked up a ball-launching machine to its maximum and could only laugh as the ball zipped by me before I could intercept it. It took a couple dozen zips before I could meet the ball with my racquet. My perception had to recalibrate. McCrone points out that we anticipate more than visually:

> For example, when we reach out for the gleaming brass handle of a door, our brain will not only be predicting the instant of contact and the correct angle at which to hold our hand, but it will also be second-guessing how the handle should actually feel as we touch it. It will be predicting the sensory parts of the experience. The fact that we are riding such a wave of predictions would soon be brought home to us if we were to reach out and discover that the handle was made of something sticky or mushy. At some subconscious level, we would already have formed the expectation of touching cold, unyielding metal. Indeed, if someone on the other side of the door happened to snatch open the door at the moment our fingers were about to close on

the handle, we might even catch a ghostly impression of what we were just about to feel with our hands. We would experience the fleeting edge of our own sensory forecast.[77]

What we think of as happening now is an anticipation of what will be happening in a fraction of second...in the near future. The prediction is based on what has been happening in the near past. Our brain does this to compensate for the fact that nerve signals take some time to travel from the sensors to the brain. If we displayed in the brain only the information we have received our display would always be off by nearly half a second. Even at a leisurely two miles per hour, things move three feet in each second. Thus our display would be a foot in error, too far off to grasp a branch or catch a ball. We don't see the ball where it is now, but where we anticipate it is now based on information from a half second prior. When things go as we guess, we don't notice anything strange because the ball is there, our hand is there, and the ball is caught.

Training, repetitive practice, muscle memory, etc. take over and the conditioned athlete can perform without deliberation. Athletes talk about being "in the zone". They are watching themselves perform the movements but not really planning them. The actions are done but not willed by them. In these sporting situations, the body takes over and calls the shots while the "person" goes along for the ride. One of the reasons people give when asked why they like to play a sport is that the activity frees them from thinking. Their consciousness is not fast enough to influence the situation so they can relax and enjoy it.

Ongoing Research on Backward Masking etc.

Connected to our impression of the flow of time is an interesting phenomenon called "backward masking," in which an initial stimulus can be blocked out of consciousness by another stimulus if the second stimulus follows the first within a couple tenths of a second. It works for pictures, sounds, or touches. The first stimulus would have reached consciousness had the second stimulus not blocked it. For example: an image of a black disk is followed quickly by an image of an encircling black ring. Only the ring will be seen if the time delay is about a tenth of a second.

Backward masking experiments continue to inform us about the complex biological activity behind consciousness. It is clear that some sensory input, which would have reached consciousness, can be suppressed after the fact by a suitable stimulus. Something later suppresses something earlier. At first it was not clear whether this is due to a suppression of memory of the event or to its appearance in consciousness. However, recent experiments show that the masked information can influence a person's behavior even though they have no conscious sense of it.

Researchers of this topic suggest that our immediate experience of "now" may extend about the length of sensory memory...a few seconds. I sometimes use this memory to review what went wrong when playing tennis. After a missed shot, if I stop and quickly pay attention to the previous action, doing a sort of instant replay, I can recall what I saw or felt in those few seconds. Perhaps I might see that I took my eye off the ball to look for my opponent's position. Waiting even a few seconds makes this trick impossible. Edelman talks about the "remembered present," a cognitive present that is a bit longer, perhaps half a minute. What we regard as "now" seems to be a collection of inputs spread out over almost a second. The immediacy of experience is an illusion.

It is now clear to researchers that not all the light that hits the retina is registered in consciousness. Some stimulus, called the target stimulus, can be suppressed by other stimuli, which interfere with the process leading to the target stimulus reaching the conscious level. There have been many techniques developed to investigate this: backward masking, forward masking, forward degraded stimulation, visual crowding, bistable figures, binocular rivalry, motion-induced blindness, attentional blink, inattentional blindness, and change blindness.

chapter

SEVEN

More Subtle Clues from Binding, Intentionality, and Camouflage

Our brain does an enormous amount of processing on sensory information before the result reaches the conscious level. Looking out the window, there is a chair, nearby a bench, beyond that a shed, then another bush, a distant tree, a far mountain. Before I know it, my brain groups the information into separate objects, identifies them (as chair, bench etc.), and locates them in a visual landscape. Philosophers have terms—"binding" and "intentionality"—to refer to aspects of this process. Intentionality (aboutness), from the Latin *intendo*, "to point to," says that in our conscious experience we tag some phenomena as "out there" and others as "in here" (thought, feelings). The term binding refers to the properties of the "out there" items. The brain identifies various properties—edges, surfaces, textures, colors, shapes, movement, sound, odor—and it binds these properties together so that we experience, not separate properties, but objects that are whole and complete in themselves. Intentionality refers to our ability to see things as not us, "out there." The illusion is so good we think it is real. But camouflage provides a clue that this isn't so.

The Army has found that when familiar objects (planes, tanks, people) are painted in irregular fashion with various colors to break up their normal shape, often an observer will fail to bind the sensory input and the object will not be seen. Binding refers to the process whereby the brain collects the details that comprise an object and correctly identifies them as belonging together, as forming a single object. The brain binds a subset of the sensory information into one object, and presents it in consciousness as one thing. All this important work is done before the sensory information reaches the conscious level. But camouflage can fool the brain and thus is a subtle clue as to how the objects that populate our brainscape are somehow constructed by the brain from sensory information about things like edges, color, orientation, and movement.

Clues from the Unseen Gorilla

We can find clues in experiments that test the reliability of eyewitness accounts of controlled events. One test uses students in a classroom. An instructor is at the front of the class talking when suddenly a person (really an actor) bursts into the room, performs some rapid series of moves (say, waves a brown stick around) and exits. The students are then asked to report what they saw. It is remarkable how poorly they perform as witnesses. A man with a dark pullover ski mask might be seen as a black man, a brown stick might be reported as a gun. Policemen have shot people offering a wallet for identification when they perceived a man extending a gun.[78]

In a remarkable variant on the theme, an audience (often students) is instructed to view a film and count the number of times a basketball is thrown from one person to another. The witnesses are thus disposed to keep an eye on the ball. But that is not the point. In the film, while balls are being tossed, a person in a gorilla suit enters the scene, jumps about waving his arms, and exits. The question to the students then is not how many tosses, but did you see the gorilla! Typically about one half fail to notice the gorilla. When the same film is rerun, some of the witnesses refuse to believe it is the same—they are so sure they would have noticed that gorilla. They were not disposed to see a gorilla, so they saw no gorilla.[79]

Even normal people with good vision can fail to consciously perceive what is occurring before their eyes. Events can take us by surprise, or we can be disposed in some other direction and fail to register in consciousness what has happened.

This is a big clue, that what we see is not the actual event but an internal representation that occurs after much unconscious brain processing.

Clues from Unconscious Activity

A more everyday clue to this unconscious brain processing is our ability to drive a car while thinking about or attending to something entirely unrelated. Preoccupied, we can drive competently for miles, avoiding other cars, stopping for lights, but sometimes missing our intended exit. If we suddenly snap back to driving consciousness, we may be unable to recount what transpired on the drive. We were driving like zombies while we were engrossed in other things like the conversation or music on the radio. Perhaps we were conscious at the time but failed to put it into memory, or perhaps we drove without consciousness being involved.

I have often had the experience, while driving, of suddenly realizing that another car has a license plate with my initials on it. I'm not aware of scanning license plates; I don't think I'm looking for my initials, but— pop, there they are! It's a good clue that our visual system does a lot of work before our consciousness is informed.

Clues from Injured Brains

Paying attention to how abilities are lost when the brain suffers injury can give us good clues about how our brainscape is created. When a part of the brain that processes visual information is damaged, the person becomes blind in part of their visual field. For example, if the damage has affected their left visual field, when objects are presented to them on the left side they will respond by saying they don't see anything there. However, if forced to make a guess or choose from a list of things that might have been presented, they are remarkably accurate in their "guesses." Their eyes still work, object identification functions still work, but somehow the information collected is not getting into the conscious brainscape. Yet some knowledge of the object is having an influence. Their hunches are good. This phenomenon is now called blindsight.[80] It is a clue that what we experience is due to brain activity. In this case it is a lack of conscious experience coupled with an accurate "gut feeling" that provides our clue.

Since my primary goal is to discuss clues available to most people, I won't be doing much with brain injury evidence. There are many fascinating books on the subject that point out the connection between localized brain damage and the loss of specific brain function[81]. Neuroscientists can identify areas associated with speech, hearing, vision, motor control, and many other functions. For example, Antonio Damasio does an excellent job of sharing how injuries reveal the brain's role in adding emotion to our inner experience. Damasio reminds us that the brain in doing its work, pulls together related sensory input, binding them together into what we perceive as a single object, and tagging it with emotion. Perhaps the item is tagged as dangerous, cute, strange, or familiar. One fascinating case, discussed by Damasio, is that of a man with a brain injury that left him able to visually recognize faces, but unable to tag them with emotion. Upon seeing his mother, he could identify her correctly, but said that he did not feel that she actually was his mother. She seemed to be an imposter. The person looked like his mother, but she now did not produce in him the familiar feeling of warmth and love. The disconnection was only for the visual pathway, however. Talking to her on the phone, hearing her voice, still connected him with the feeling of "this is my mother".

Another patient, Emily, suffered damage to her brain's face area, and as a result she could not recognize her own face in the mirror. However, she could immediately recognize her own voice when played back from a tape recorder. She could tag her voice as her own but not her image. That is, she could add the emotion of "this is me" to her voice but not to her image.

Sometimes when meeting someone for the first time and noticing an initial attraction (or repulsion), I can uncover how they resemble some other person I like (or dislike). We can transfer emotional tags from one person to another based on the similarity of their characteristics (hairstyle, voice, body shape, etc.). This profiling or stereotyping can cause problems in relationships but when we can see it operating it is a good clue as to how the brain adds emotion to our inner world.

Recently in the news, two young teenage girls stirred up the emotions of older people by wearing T-shirts modifying the common happy face design to look like Hitler.

It is difficult for me to suppress strong negative emotions when seeing the swastika symbol, even when it is part of an American Indian design. Our culture conditions us to respond to hundreds of symbols—the cross, star of David, stars and stripes, rising sun, crescent moon and star, raised middle finger, thumbs down, OK sign, dollar sign, and so on. Volumes have been written on the subject, but our clue is to observe it happening—the symbol evoking emotion. Emotion is not "out there". As with all that we experience it is in our brainscape. It is in here—WYSIRY.

Clues from Super Senses

Another clue to the personal nature of our internal experience is when we encounter people with superior senses. Consider people with perfect pitch. Some people have a remarkable ability to remember and identify musical tones. Play a note on a piano or guitar, and they can name it. In my twenties, recognizing that I was musically retarded, I bought a guitar in the hopes of educating myself but I had difficulty tuning it. I got a tuning fork but when I sounded it against a guitar note, although I could hear the tones were different, I could not tell which was higher. Luckily at that time I had a friend with perfect pitch, and she would help me tune my guitar over the phone. Her tonal gift was not all positive though. She said she found it unpleasant to listen to most music because the instruments were out of tune. She listened to only a few perfect recordings. Her aural world was different from mine. I imagine it to be richer in tonal detail, with complex harmonies and disharmonies. All of us have different physical structures, externally and internally, and this can lead to different brainscapes. We each construct our phenomenal world in our own unique way.

I notice, as my sense of balance worsens, that some people have what could be called perfect balance. Ballet dancers balance on point. Gymnasts perform handstands on the rings. They also seem to have perfect proprioception—they know where in space their bodies are. Other people have perfect taste or perfect smell, at least compared to most of us. I have a friend who, as a young man, had perfect vision. We would test ourselves against him by reading print from a distance. He would start reading at 30 feet what most of us could read at 15 feet—and he was equally superior at short-distance reading. Alas, he now wears glasses.

Some people have eidetic (photographic) memories. There is a man named Kim Peek[82] who was born without the connection between the two hemispheres of his brain, the corpus callosum. He has read and memorized 9,000 books. When reading a book, Peek reads the left page with his left eye and the right page with his right eye, a strong clue that his brain is organized differently from most brains. Memory, of course, is not a sense, but Peek's amazing talent points to vast differences in how human brains can function. The assumption that our inner experience of the world is the same as everyone else's is not justified. Our brainscapes are most likely quite idiosyncratic, a private blend of sensory input, colored by our unique emotions, thoughts, and memories.

Clues from the Body map

What can we say about the brainscape? To reiterate, it is that of which we are conscious. All our sensory input—sight, sound, smell, taste, touch, etc.,—combines to create our internal display of what is outside of us. In this display there are parts that we feel are "not us." These parts are not permanent—the walls, the ceiling, the floor. They are not permanent in the sense that they are not always there; these impermanent parts are not present when we are at the beach. Our feeling is that these parts are "out there," "not mine."[83]

But some parts are always present; our legs, thighs, chest, arms, hands and shoulders, can be easily seen. Of the head we see only the side of the nose (one side with each eye), some of the lips and cheek and the edge of the eye sockets. We can't see our neck, ears, or the top and back of our head but we can feel these parts. We can wiggle our ears or scrunch up our scalp and get a feel for the parts of head and body that we don't see. We have a good sense of the volume of our body that we feel as "mine."[84]

In our brainscape we have both a sensory and motor image of our body and head. But this head in our phenomenal experience, which we partly see and mostly feel, is really an image of our head that is taking place in our head! More correctly it is an impression of a head that is created in the brain. This head, which we partially see in our field of view, does not have our brain inside of it. It is the other way around: our brain has in it a representation of our head. In this representation, the image of the head is useful for displaying proprioceptive information about the position of the head: is the head erect, is it tilted or rotated with respect to the chest, etc. But, and here is the point that amazes me, the brain is not located inside this private representation of the head. If your belief is that your thoughts, feelings (felts), and memories are occurring inside this head, then perhaps you also feel that "you" are inside the part of your brainscape that is your head or body. But that is not correct.

Your brain makes a brainscape that consists of an image of the world that contains an image of your body in that world. Your brain is not located inside the image of the head. In a manner of speaking, your brain is everywhere in the scene. The scene is not "before you", the scene is "within you"—but it is not within the image of you.

Trees are correctly located in our brainscape as being outside our body, but where should we locate thinking? Thinking takes place in the brain, but where in the brainscape are the brain and thinking to be located? In a way, this is similar to the situation of having to coordinate what we see with our tactile sense. The vision and touch systems have different input—from the eyes and skin. We learn to bind them together, but as the rubber hand demonstration shows, this coordination is easily led astray.

How can we locate our thinking in the brainscape? With our eyes closed we have some sense of where our limbs are because we have proprioceptive feedback to give such information to the brain. But there is no such proprioception for thinking. We have no reason to locate thinking in one part of the brainscape rather than another. Yet most of us, I would guess, tend to locate our thinking and imagination in that volume of our brainscape that we assign to the head.

If I ask you where your thinking is happening (where your self is) you might point to your head, and from my external vantage point that is understandable. However, if I pose this question to myself, if I ask where in my inner world I am to locate my thinking (and my "self"), then the previous answer is not correct. Perhaps a sweeping gesture with my hand, to indicate everywhere in the brainscape, is more appropriate. It is incorrect to conceive of thinking as taking place within the brainscape's image of the head, i.e. in "your" head. In your own private representation of reality, which includes a representation of your body and head, there is nothing special happening in that head. It is not correct to feel you are located in your head a few inches behind your eyes. Another person looking at you would be correct to say, "You are in this head that I see." But, seen from the inside (subjectively that is), the head you see, which you feel to be yours, does not contain you.

This is an important point, so let us approach it a bit differently. When we look around at the world, we are certainly examining our internal representation of what our senses bring to us. We see objects and usually some parts of our bodies. Some of the things in our representation are tagged with the feeling of "not me", and some are tagged as "me." Of course there is no label sticking to each thing but, as we look at the various things, we feel connected to some and unconnected to others. The thought of stapling the paper is far less stressful than that of stapling the hand. The tagging is accomplished at a sub conscious level. We just observe it.

Knowing how sensory nerves connect to the brain, we realize the representation is intimately involved with the brain. It is taking place within the brain. Within this representation there is a representation of our head. This representation of our head is occurring in our brain, but it does not contain the brain. The head in our brainscape is empty; there is no self (or anything else) in it.[85] It is very much like looking at a photo of your head. You will find nothing going on inside that photo-head, nor do you expect to find anything. Also, when we look at a mirror and see an image of our head, we do not think anything is happening inside that head. But somehow we do expect to find something going on inside the head we (partially) see with our eyes open, the head displayed in our brainscape.

Cartoonists sometimes use a bubble to indicate what is going on inside a cartoon character's head:

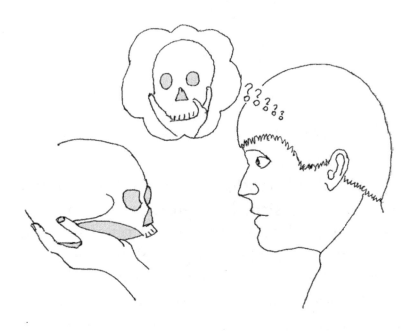

The above cartoon is very simple. Perhaps the following one is closer to our situation:

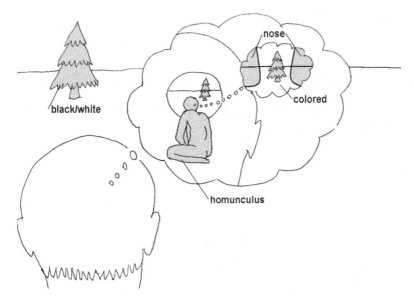

What this cartoon is meant to portray is someone, standing erect, looking at a tree. I would guess that most people, who have never really thought about perception, feel that something in them is peering out through their eyes. This is largely an unconscious idea, sketched above as a little person looking out of an eye. They make a mistake to think it is this little person who sees. What the homunculus sees is represented by the second bubble. In this case you can't see your legs or torso, just a partial glimpse of your nose, cheeks, and eyebrows, seen in a partially overlapping view through the left and right eyes. This is what we see. The rest of our body and head is added via tactile proprioceptive sensations and cannot be sketched. The external world is labeled as black/white—only the brainscape is in color.

We may feel our head is there due to a breeze on the hair, coolness on the skin, pressure of the eyeglasses, etc, and thus the head is represented in consciousness. This head in our image has nothing going on inside of it, but we have been led to imagine that this is where we exist…behind our eyes, peering out. Steve Lehar's website has wonderful drawings to illustrate this.[86]

Perhaps we can conclude this section by continuing our imagined conversation between Socrates and Glaucon.

Glaucon: Earlier you pointed out that at the center of my virtual world is an image of my body. I can see my legs and torso but only parts of my nose, cheekbones, and eyebrows. However-er, I can reach up and touch and feel my head.

Socrates: And where in all this imagery do you locate your brain?

Glaucon: I have been taught that the brain is in the skull, so I might once have said the brain is in the image of the skull, that is, the head...or at least what I can see of it. But that is where the image of the brain would be found...and I don't really have any image of the brain. It seems more a thought that the brain exists behind the eyes, so to speak.

Socrates: That being so...where is your actual brain?

Glaucon: Since the virtual world is in the brain, the brain would envel-op and encompass it. And the skull would lie outside the largest volume of our sight.[87]

Socrates: That is the situation. And in all this, where do you locate your thoughts—and your self, for that matter?

Glaucon: Certainly not in that small imagined volume behind the eyes. We have no reason or sensory input to confine thought, our self, to this small region. We must consider thought to be found everywhere in this vast virtual world.

Socrates: Consider it you have...but why so silent now?

Glaucon: It is really shocking to see all this...to see life in a different way. I had not thought about life in these terms before, but if you had forced me to respond I would have said I am in my body, or perhaps, in my head, which in turn is contained in, surrounded by, a real world of colorful objects, sounds, textures, smells, etc. But now I see this cannot be the case and I must learn to live with a different view of my self and the world.

Socrates: So have we all to learn this new way.

chapter

EIGHT

"First of all, then, I ask, What does the expression 'mystical states of consciousness' mean? How do we part off mystical states from other states?"
—William James

The previous chapter ends with an imagined dialog between Socrates and Glaucon where we hear that we all have to learn a new way of seeing our life. This would be the "examined life" that Socrates feels gives meaning to our existence. It begins when we appreciate that we cannot directly see or touch the real world around us but come to know of its presence through our senses. We then create a model of that world. The model is created by our brain and is in our brain, in the same way that a dream is in our brain. We have examined many clues that point to this being the case, that what you see is really you. But have all these clues really convinced you in more than an intellectual way? Have they produced any change in the way you now see the world? After all, that is what Socrates is aiming for.

Is it even possible for us to see the world in a different way? To really grasp that the world, which seems to be out there, in front of us, is occurring in us? That what we take to be our body is a proxy for our body in our internal brainscape? Can we comprehend the essence of this. The brain processes that produce the illusion (our brainscape) go on without entering consciousness. The processes are invisible to us, they are "transparent" as Metzinger says. At the risk of copyright infringement, here is a rather long quote from Metzinger.[88]

> Still, it is true to say that phenomenal experience as such unfolds in an *internal* space, in a space quite distinct from the world described by ordinary physics. It evolves within an individual model of reality, in an individual organism's brain, and its experiential properties are determined exclusively by properties within this brain. Although this simple fact may well be cognitively available to many of us, we are neurophenomenological cavemen in that none of us are able to consciously experience its truth. Effortlessly, we enjoy an "out-of-the-brain experience." Only if confronted with the data and discoveries of modern neuropsychology, or if pressed to come up with a convincing argument showing that currently we are *not* just a shadow on the wall of the phenomenal cave generated by some sort of isolated, minimally sufficient correlate stimulated by an evil scientist, only then do we sometimes begin to devel-

op a stronger intuitive sense of what it means that our phenomenal model of reality is an *internal* model of reality that could at any time, in principle, turn out to be quite far removed from a much more high-dimensional physical reality than we have ever thought of. Plato, however, tells us there is an entrance to the cave, which at the same time may be a potential exit. But who could it be? Who could ever pass *through* this exit?

In Plato's beautiful parable the captives in the cave are chained down by their thighs and necks. They have been in this position since birth, and they can only look straight ahead, because even their head has been in a fixed position from the beginning of their existence onward. They are prevented by their fetters from turning their heads. As Socrates points out, they have never seen anything of themselves and each other except the shadows cast by the fire burning behind them to the opposite wall of the cave, and which they take for real objects. The same is true of the objects carried along above the low wall behind their heads. What is the cave? The cave, according to SMT [Metzinger's self-model theory], is simply the physical organism as a whole, including, in particular, its brain. What are the shadows on the wall? A shadow is a low-dimensional projection of a higher-dimensional object. *Phenomenal* shadows are low-dimensional projections of internal or external objects in the conscious state space opened within the central nervous system of a biological organism. According to the SMT, the shadows on the wall are phenomenal mental models. The book you are holding in your hands, as consciously experienced by you at this moment, is a dynamic, low-dimensional shadow of the actual physical object in your hand, a dancing shadow in your central nervous system. As all neural modelers know, real-life connectionist systems typically achieve a major reduction in the dimensionality of their input vectors at the very first processing stage, when transforming the activation pattern on their sensory surface into the first hidden layer. But what is the fire, causing the projection of flickering shadows of consciousness, ever changing, dancing away as activation patterns on the surface of your neural cave? The fire is neural dynamics. The fire is the incessant, self-regulating flow of neural information processing, constantly perturbed and modulated by sensory and cognitive input. The wall is not a *two-dimensional* surface. It is a *space*, namely, the high-dimensional phenomenal state space of human technicolor phenomenology (see McGinn 1989, p. 349; Metzinger 2000, p. 1f.) Please note that, in a conscious human being, the wall and the fire are not separate entities: they are two aspects of one and the same process. But what exactly does it mean when Plato tells us that we have never seen anything of ourselves but our *own* shadow on the opposite wall? It means that, as perceiving, attending, thinking, and even as acting subjects, we are only given to ourselves through what I have called the PSM— the phenomenal self-model. Could we free ourselves from our attachment to this inner image of ourselves, the dancing shadow in our conscious state space? Could we stop to *confuse* ourselves with this shadow, and leave Plato's cave altogether?

What would it be like for a person to leave the cave? Mother Nature has taken billions of years to evolve creatures, like us, that are adapted to life in the cave. In Plato's cave, the captive person mistakes the shadow of the body for the actual body. She also mistakes the shadow of things for the actual things. Leaving the cave would imply she gains insight into shadows, and now see them as proxies for the real objects, each created by the same process. Although we can never leave the cave of the skull we ask: Can we see the objects of our phenomenal world, including our body image, as proxies?

We can expect this to be a difficult task. This ability we all have to collect information from out there and construct a model of the world from it is not something we have learned but rather something we have inherited. The ability is built into us. With it we have also inherited the capacity to distinguish what is us from what is not us. When we look around the phenomenal world we clearly see the soil and our feet and just know which is which. The feelings of, "this is me" or "this is not me" come with the territory, so to speak. It could be maladaptive to change to a altered state of being where these inherited abilities are questioned. It could reduce our ability to survive in the world. However, we can still ask the question: What could be the characteristics of such an altered state? Let us speculate.

First, the sense of separation between self and other might vanish. The speculation here is that the brain might get some inkling of the process that is generating both self and other. Or to put it another way, the usually invisible (transparent) process that is producing the objects of the brainscape might rise to the conscious level. Should that happen, self and other might no longer feel different, as they would be seen to have a common origin. Even the once clear distinctions between objects, chair v.s. table v.s. book, might soften. A feeling of homogeneity or oneness might be experienced. The same brain process is making all these phenomena, so in a way they are all the same (i.e. they are all products of the brain). The brain, of course, does not know it is a brain but it might, we are speculating, get some glimpse of the formerly invisible process that is going on. The process might become opaque.

A second characteristic of an altered state might be an altered sense of time similar to the way we lose track of time when we are engrossed in some favored activity. Having a sense of the passage of time seems to require us putting some trace of what is happening into memory. Presumably we do this in some shorthand way, recording only salient aspects of what has occurred, rather than recording faithfully the input of all the senses. In this altered state we might not recognize the salient features (table, chair, book), so recording it would be very difficult. Without the usual memory trace, it might seem timeless. Or at least the sense of time would be different from our normal sense.

A third characteristic of an altered state might occur after the state had worn off. One might be left with the sense that something profound had occurred. After all, the altered state is very different from the normal state. Imagine a person living their entire life in the normal state of being and then suddenly in an altered state where the reality of objects is in question. The sense of self is in question. This could be felt as something very deep, very profound. Depending on the person's background, the state could be profoundly elevating or profoundly depressing.

A fourth characteristic of an altered state might be its ineffability. Because of the difficulty of capturing features of the state in memory, the person would have difficulty talking about the experience or even trying to grasp what had occurred for themselves. How could one talk about a state that is so removed from ordinary reality? Perhaps only the feelings that accompanied the altered state could be recalled. Feelings of homogeneity, oneness, timelessness, or profoundness would be accessible. All of which are difficult to put into words—ineffable.

Can a person who has not had such an out-of-the-cave experience nonetheless get some glimpse into the feelings of homogeneity, oneness, timelessness, and profundity of which we speak. Metzinger suggests the state of lucid dreaming might have characteristics similar to the state we are trying to understand. Here is a quote with which Stephen LaBerge begins *Lucid Dreaming*:

> I realized I was dreaming. I raised my arms and began to rise (actually I was being lifted). I rose through black sky that blended to indigo, to deep purple, to lavender, to white, then to very bright light. All the time I was being lifted there was the most beautiful music I have ever heard. It seemed like voices rather than instruments.

There are no words to describe the JOY I felt. I was very gently lowered back to earth. I had the feeling that I had come to a turning point in my life and I had chosen the right path. The dream, the joy I experienced, was kind of a reward, or so I felt. It was a long, slow slide back to wakefulness with the music echoing in my ears. The euphoria lasted several days; the memory forever.—A. F., Bay City, Michigan

This is an example of a lucid dream, in which the dreamer realizes he is dreaming. In the dream he has a sense of being embodied, yet he knows that his body is not his real body, it is a dream-body. Of course, in realizing he is dreaming, he realizes that all the dream objects are his dream creation. The profundity of the experience is obvious in his capitalization of the word JOY, in the euphoria and lasting memory. The ineffability is in the phrase "there are no words to describe".

Perhaps we all have memories of ordinary dreams (non-lucid) with similar incidents. But the lucid dream, in which we know it is a dream while we are dreaming, is more to the point. While dreaming we know it is not real. Our dream-body is not our body. The dream-objects are not real objects. In that way it is like our speculation as to what it might be like to realize that what we see around us is a kind of waking dream.

Hopefully you can see where I am going with all this. For comparison, here is a quote from William James's *Varieties of Religious Experience*. He is describing one of his many examples of the mystical experience:

> One brilliant Sunday morning, my wife and boys went to the Unitarian Chapel in Macclesfield. I felt it impossible to accompany them—as though to leave the sunshine on the hills, and go down there to the chapel, would be for the time an act of spiritual suicide. And I felt such need for new

inspiration and expansion in my life. So, very reluctantly and sadly, I left my wife and boys to go down into the town, while I went further up into the hills with my stick and my dog. In the loveliness of the morning, and the beauty of the hills and valleys, I soon lost my sense of sadness and regret. For nearly an hour I walked along the road to the "Cat and Fiddle," and then returned. On the way back, suddenly, without warning, I felt that I was in Heaven—an inward state of peace and joy and assurance indescribably intense, accompanied with a sense of being bathed in a warm glow of light, as though the external condition had brought about the internal effect—a feeling of having passed beyond the body, though the scene around me stood out more clearly and as if nearer to me than before, by reason of the illumination in the midst of which I seemed to be placed. This deep emotion lasted, though with decreasing strength, until I reached home, and for some time after. Only gradually passing away.

Read again this quote from James: "First of all, then, I ask, What does the expression 'mystical states of consciousness' mean? How do we part off mystical states from other states?" He goes on to propose four marks which, when an experience has them, may justify us in calling it mystical.

1. *Ineffability.* The subject of it immediately says that it defies expression, that no adequate report of its contents can be given in words. It follows from this that its quality must be directly experienced; it cannot be imparted or transferred to others. In this peculiarity mystical states are more like states of feeling than like states of intellect.

2. *Noetic Quality.* They are states of insight into depths of truth unplumbed by the discursive intellect. They are illuminations, revelations, full of significance and importance, all inarticulate though they remain; and as a rule they carry with them a curious sense of authority for after-time.

3. *Transiency.* Mystical states cannot be sustained for long. Except in rare instances, half an hour, or at most an hour or two, seems to be the limit beyond which they fade into the light of common day. Often, when faded, their quality can but imperfectly be reproduced in memory; but when they recur it is recognized; and from one recurrence to another it is susceptible of continuous development in what is felt as inner richness and importance.

4. *Passivity.* The mystic feels as if his own will were in abeyance, and indeed sometimes as if he were grasped and held by a superior power....Mystical states, strictly so called, are never merely interruptive. Some memory of their content always remains, and a profound sense of their importance.

What I am suggesting is that the state of seeing into our brain process, the state of lucid dreaming, and the mystical state are related—the state of lucid dreaming being similar to a mind getting an inkling of its unconscious working, and both of these states being similar to the state of mystical experience. I am suggesting this understanding to be a kind of bridge between the material world and the spiritual world. Some people seem to be such firm materialists that any suggestion of mystical or spiritual experiences raises their blood pressure. Other people are such strong spiritual types that any suggestion that mystical states are anything other than proof of a spiritual world causes them to withdraw. These two types of people, multiplied by billions, have been battling for centuries. The materialists fail to recognize the trick played on them by their own brain—WYSIRY. But the spiritualists fail to recognize the same thing. They do not comprehend how the brain creates the phenomenal world in which we seem to live. Here is the bridge to common ground. When we realize that we live in a cave, that our world and our selves are a phenomena created by our brain, perhaps we can use this powerful understanding to soften our divisions.

Speaking to materialists: Can you appreciate how our phenomenal world, which somehow rides on the material brain, has spiritual properties? You can't grasp it, or measure it with instruments. You can't see it or be sure of it's existence in other people or animals, but we live as though others have an internal life similar to ours. Getting a sense of the truth of this is a kind of mystical experience.

Speaking to spiritualists: Can you appreciate how our brains, material things no doubt, create an internal brainscape with many characteristics of a spiritual world? Perhaps the spiritual world you believe in is all around you. Your brainscape is a spiritual world. Getting a sense of this is a mystical experience.

There have been, and still are, many different religions that influence our lives. My understanding is that the origin of each one can be traced to some person who has had a mystical experience. The experience sets them apart from others and serves as the seed for what grows out of it. The various experiences are similar, I claim, but the interpretations they and their followers give to the experiences are very different. Some followers many have had similar experiences and help propagate the group. Others are attracted by the group interpretation or the character of the leader. But groups clash and fight and many people have died in support of their religion. The conflicts continue to create uncertainty and fear even today.

My hope is that understanding that the scene around us is actually in us will become common knowledge—just as everyone now knows the earth is round and not flat, and that it orbits the Sun. When this profound fact of physiology is shared by all, there will be correspondingly profound changes in our society. Changes, I hope, for the better.

chapter

NINE

What Is Consciousness?

Plato's Parable of the Cave Breaks Down

Plato's parable of the cave is an analogy of our situation with respect to the world outside of us. Every analogy breaks down if pushed too far. In physics, the first analogy for an atom of matter was the idea of an indestructible lump, *a—tom* in Greek means "not cut." Much later the analogy of a planet orbiting the sun was invoked for the electron and nucleus. These analogies were useful at first, but at some later time they failed to correspond to experiment. In science, verbal analogies have given way to mathematical analogies, but they too have their limitations. Analogies are more like pointers or signposts. When you see a sign that reads "BEACH" you use it to change direction and head off toward the beach.

Where does Plato's analogy of the person chained in the cave break down? In Plato's cave the shadows on the wall are related to the world outside the cave and this is an excellent pointer to our shadows (the brainscape) being related to a world external to our body. But this analogy breaks down when we try to find what it is in us that corresponds to the captive chained in Plato's cave. There is no little person in our brain looking at the image, the brainscape, that the brain generates.

We think of conscious experience as being in the brain because of our accumulated understanding of brain structure and function. We have learned how the eye sends signals to the brain via the optic nerve, the ear via the auditory nerve, and similarly for all the sensors of the body. All connect to the brain. We also know that even severe damage to the arms, legs, liver, kidney, or heart do not affect the ability to have conscious experience. But damage to even minute parts of the brain can halt the conscious experience. Many people have had organ transplants and yet they remain the same person. No person has received a brain transplant yet, but I assume that if that ever were to occur there would be a major change in the experience of the recipient. As someone said, "In a brain transplant, it is better to be the donor than the recipient." The brain is central to the conscious experience. The quantity of evidence from research that points to the brain as the organ of consciousness is now impressive. The body may be intact and functioning but if the brain is dead the person is gone. The brain connects with the world through the senses via nerve fibers and receives informative chemical signals. Then in some way not fully understood, consciousness emerges. A phenomenal representation of the world arises, and the observer is represented in that presentation. The phenomenal representation is in the brain but we fail to appreciate this fact. Thus it is said that the image is in the brain.

We also understand that we do not know *where* in the brain consciousness happens. Most brain researchers have given up on the notion that it all comes together in some small spot in the brain. Consciousness involves a larger portion of the brain, but we do not know where. We also do not know how the brain generates conscious experience. This is the big mystery, the "hard problem."[89] How is the connection between the current physical state of my brain related to the subjective experience that accompanies that brain state? Scientists could, if they had much better instruments, measure the state of my brain, but only I could report on what exactly is occurring in my conscious experience at the time of measurement. Perhaps it may even turn out to be like the well-known Heisenberg uncertainty principle. Increasingly accurate measurements of the state of my brain might begin to alter that brain state and change my experience during the act of measurement. No one has any idea how physical matter, organic or inorganic, can produce the qualities we experience in our phenomenal presentation... the colors, sounds, tastes etc. This leads many to take the position that it will always remain an unfathomable mystery. The explanatory gap is too wide. This is the "hard problem." Many people feel we will never bridge the worlds of reality and phenomenal experience.

Perhaps, after many brain measurements and with true reports of my experience, a correspondence could be found between every brain state and its correlate in consciousness. Although correlation is not explanation, some researchers think this is the best we will ever be able to achieve. The state of the brain is linked to a reported state of consciousness. Some of these researchers view it this way: The brain state does not cause consciousness, rather the brain state *is* consciousness. The brain state and consciousness are inseparable. The brain state is what you see when you examine the brain from the outside, and consciousness is what you see when looking from the inside.

Philosophers have a word to refer to this kind of brain/consciousness connection—supervenience. This is suggesting that if my brain is in a state now that is the same as some earlier state then my conscious experience now will be the same as the earlier experience—and vice versa. This principle is not an explanation of consciousness. To say that certain configurations of matter, brain states, are conscious begs the question, "What is consciousness?" Alas, it is the best we can do for now and maybe for all time.

Consciousness and Electromagnetism

How does the brain produce consciousness? Of course, no one knows. The most popular approach right now is to implicate the neurons in some sort of orchestrated activity that causes us to be conscious. The suggestion is that groups or layers of neurons receive input (nerve signals) from higher and lower layers and in turn produce output to those and other layers. Brain researchers are trying to map the elaborate mapping of communication between neurons in the brain. But there is no compelling explanation as to how all this activity would produce, for example, the visual and auditory experiences we have when awake or when dreaming.

The nervous system is a collection of specialized cells (neurons, glial cells, etc.) organized in a complex manner, communicating with each other via electrochemical signals. A common postulate of brain researchers is that consciousness is a result of the dynamic pulsation of this vast, essentially electrical, assemblage. This is, of course, not an explanation of consciousness, but it does postulate an essential correlation of consciousness with the functioning of complex configurations of neurons.

Even if we accept that systems of neurons can give rise to consciousness, we can still ask what it is about neurons that causes consciousness to happen.

Our consciousness seems to be very closely tied to electromagnetism. We routinely measure the brain's electric and magnetic activity by placing electrodes on the scalp in a non-invasive way and using the electroencephalograph (EEG) and magnetoencephalograph (MEG). We measure heart activity in a similar way via electrodes on the chest. The electrical conductivity of the skin, galvanic skin response, is the basis of the lie detector. It is interesting to speculate that perhaps our brand of consciousness is some sort of electromagnetic phenomenon—of course viewed from the inside. The brain, by setting up some configuration of neurons, sets up a complex charge configuration, which of course has an electromagnetic field associated with it. It is tempting to say that this electromagnetic field supervenes upon the charge configuration. Thus the function of the brain is to handle and manipulate charge to control consciousness. The charges under consideration would be the negative electrons and various positive and negative ions of our chemical milieu.

There is one other aspect of electromagnetism that has a parallel with consciousness. Electric and magnetic fields have electric charges as their source. But we cannot see these fields directly and can only observe their effects on other electric particles (charges). Similarly, consciousness seems to have a source in brain matter and "surrounds" it like some "field of consciousness." We cannot observe consciousness directly (except our own) and must be content with observing its affect on (brain) matter. The electric field is like a spirit connected to earthly charges. Consciousness is like a spirit connected to the earthly brain matter.

Consciousness and Artificial Intelligence

Similar to our brains, computers also control the flow of charge by use of transistor circuits embedded in silicon chips. Perhaps if an appropriate program were run on a computer a conscious charge configuration could be established. In this case, the program would not be conscious but the electromagnetic configuration it establishes might be conscious.

The photo diode that opens a door for you or turns on a light or adjusts your camera's exposure is certainly sensitive to light, but does it have a flash of consciousness as it senses the light? Of course we don't know, but all but the most careful of philosophers would say it does not. How about an array of millions of such detectors passing their information to some pattern recognition program that voices your name as you approach? Is this enough to be conscious? Again, probably not.

What if we constructed a robot that could see, hear, talk, and remember as well as we do? Would it be conscious? Here is where many say, " Yes, this robot is as conscious as I am." This is, of course, the underlying belief in the field of artificial intelligence, AI. But many argue that such a robot still would not be conscious.[90] It is just an elaborate machine with no "show" going on inside, a lifeless Zombie. But saying this, we would then need to ask, "What is the function of our consciousness?" If a machine that has no consciousness could do it all, what does having consciousness contribute? What is consciousness good for? These are some of the questions that philosophers struggle with.

The debate is likely to go on for many decades—or at least until such a sophisticated robot is built.

Consciousness and Other Animals

Looking from the other end, the conscious end, I am conscious and I believe my fellow humans are conscious too. We came from animals. We, like the other apes, are animals. I believe all mammals and also birds and reptiles are conscious.

Consciousness, most likely, is a biological function, like digestion and reproduction. But how about an insect or a worm or a paramecium or a plant? Consciousness in lower animals or in plants would have to be very different from human consciousness, if there were any consciousness at all, because of the lack of a developed nervous system. Perhaps critters with very simple nervous systems—or none at all—are not conscious.

Some people believe only humans are conscious, that we are special in some way. I believe these people are too anthropocentric. Compare our blueprints, our DNA, with that of our fellow creatures. All DNA is based on a helix with a right-handed twist, like a screw that advances when you twist it clockwise. No living thing has DNA that is left-handed. In addition to this, we have learned that all DNA uses the same four base units in the construction of the genetic code. This is strong evidence for the connectedness of all life.

Our DNA is about 98% similar to that of chimps, and some segments of it are also seen in worms and flies. There seems to be an increasing chain of complexity in the DNA going from older, simple organisms to those more recent and complex. More complex creatures that sport muscles, bones, nerves, and immune systems have evolved genes to support these functions. Is there some point in this increasing complexity where consciousness suddenly turns on? Does this happen at the human level? Or is it lower? Or all the way down? Of course we don't know. Many argue that a nervous system is the necessary matrix to support consciousness (and also complex subconscious activity).

A nervous system is a collection of specialized cells (neurons, glial cells, etc.) organized in a complex manner, communicating with each other via electrochemical signals. A common postulate of brain researchers is that consciousness is a result of the dynamic pulsation of this vast, essentially electrical, assemblage. This is, of course, not an explanation of consciousness, but it does postulate an essential correlation of consciousness with the functioning of complex configurations of neurons.

Consciousness and Quantum Mechanics

Some people think neurons and diodes are too coarse to account for the subtleness of consciousness[91]. They look for much smaller structures within brain cells on which to pin their hopes. Hameroff and Penrose hope that microtubles threading through our cells could provide the necessary environment for quantum mechanical effects to be supported in brains. This reminds me of the emergence of superconductivity in certain materials. The metal lead, ordinarily a poor conductor of electricity, if cooled to within a few degrees of absolute zero, undergoes a remarkable transition. Although the atomic structure does not change, the electrons within the metal somehow pair up and can then effortlessly dance around the metal atoms without losing energy. A current established in a ring of metal, if kept cold, can persist unassisted for years. This superconductivity is a quantum effect and is an emergent phenomenon. Other materials have been discovered that can do the same thing but at much higher temperatures. The record now is a copper perovskite that needs to be cooled to a mere -135 degrees Celsius (-211 Fahrenheit). A dream of these researchers is to achieve room-temperature superconductivity. Perhaps the microtubles of the brain produce some organic room-temperature quantum states, which are our conscious states. Still, there is no way that even this situation gives any explanation of the reds and blues of our experience.

The quantum suggestion has a few things in its favor. Unlike neurons, which are in one state or another, quantum states can be a superposition of many states at once. This view seems to leave room for choice and free will, which are difficult subjects for the more machine like neuronal brain states.

It is safe to say we humans are conscious, but we do not yet know what it is in us that makes us so.

Appendix

I

"To kill and error is as good a service as and sometimes even better than, the establishing of a new truth or fact."
—Charles Darwin

We Are Just Beginning To Investigate Consciousness

There is much about being a conscious being that is difficult to put into words—

the ineffable. Far too much has been said about the ineffable. Here is a brief review of the effable.

We homo sapiens started in Africa and spread out from there to Europe and Asia. Not so long ago really, we humans were very animal-like and lived in caves and among trees (100,000? years ago), we probably could speak and had used fire for many millennia. Important changes (in our brains) occurred 50,000 years ago signaled by the appearance of jewelry and art[92]. Watercraft probably were used to populate Australia 40,000 years ago but didn't appear in the Mediterranean until 13,000 years ago, about the time humans arrived in North America. Farming and domestication of animals began around 10,000 years ago (including the wheel, writing, metalworking. and beer). Glass was made in 3500 BC, the first compass around 200 BC, but the telescope, microscope and pendulum did not appear until 1600 AD. Steam power came in the 1700's followed by the industrial revolution of the 1800's. The use of electricity waited until the 1900's.

2000 years ago our Mediterranean ancestors believed their cities were the center of the universe on a flat earth. They believed all things had their place in the universe: earth at the bottom, water above earth, air above water and fire above all. Dragons and demons, angels and devils, ghosts and goblins, fairies and spirits, witches and warlocks. Since the Renaissance (1600's) there has been a gradual pruning of these branches of belief, but not all have disappeared. We are still in the midst of the process of dropping beliefs that are not fitting.

Western civilization stems from Mediterranean culture ,which, by the end of the dark ages (1500's), had forgotten the origins of the Pyramids, the Parthenon and Greek thought, and the Coliseum. Marco Polo had to "discover" the thriving culture of China, and Columbus "discovered" the New World, which had been inhabited for 13,000 years.

In the late 1800's we first came to understand the nature of light as an electromagnetic phenomenon, although we still puzzle over its wave/particle duality. Also at this time, Darwin introduces us to our connection with the primates and to all life on earth. And Freud introduced us to the unconscious parts of our behavior. Psychosomatic illness is a more recent finding. Most people no longer believe the heart to be the center of emotions, but the notion is still a powerful symbol today. The idea, now accepted wisdom, that matter is composed of atoms was still debated in the early 1900's.

We now know the universe is very old, at least 14 billion years if not infinitely old, The earth also is very old (4.6 billion years) not the 5000 years that people thought until quite recently (and of course some still insist on). We know the earth goes around the sun[93] and that the stars are distant suns[94]. We know that the matter of earth was cooked up in previous stars.

In the decade before I was born, we discovered that what we call the Milky Way Galaxy , the galaxy in which our sun and earth reside, is not the entire universe but one among billions of galaxies. Today astronomical data suggest that the distance between these galaxies is expanding[95] and that the expansion is not slowing down but is continuing to speed up. The matter we can see directly is only a few percent of the stuff of the universe. Dark matter and dark energy are terms coined to refer to the invisible majority of matter in the universe.

An important discovery that many of us remember unfolding is that of continental drift. First suggested in the early 1900's, it was not until the 1960's that the fantastic idea of continents on huge slowly moving plates was accepted by the scientific community. About the time DNA, genes, and the genetic code became were discovered. Also, the nucleus, elementary particles and nuclear energy.

In human terms, my Grandmother was born before the acceptance of the atomic theory, electricity, cars and airplanes. My Mother saw radio, movies, refrigerators, telephones and Quantum Mechanics (although she was unaware of it). In my life was born: TV, nuclear weapons, continental drift, lunar landings, microwave ovens, computers, the internet, cell phones and global warming.

The point is we humans evolved from predecessors of the apes and were at first very ignorant. We taught ourselves everything we know. We have learned a lot but we have a lot to learn, a lot to absorb into our culture. We also have much to unlearn, incorrect ideas we need to drop from our culture.

Say you are in great physical condition and could walk at 4 miles per hour for 20 hours—80 miles. Let 80 miles represent the age of the earth (about 5 billion years). On this 80 mile ruler one inch is 1000 years. If your first step represents the birth of the Earth, your last step encompasses all of human civilization and a typical person's lifetime is 1/16 of an inch. We humans have not been around very long and we have much to learn. The idea of carefully observing and measuring the world around us took root only in the last ½ inch. Making ourselves the subject of investigation is even more recent, perhaps 1/8 of an inch. We have been astoundingly ignorant of our own functioning. This has been revealed by such harmful activities as smoking, over use of alcohol, painting watch faces with radium, insulating with asbestos, using mercury in manufacturing, pollution of our water and air, and global warming. From an historical perspective we have just started to understand ourselves.

The quantity of evidence from research that points to the brain as the organ of consciousness is now impressive. The body may be intact and functioning but if the brain is dead the person is gone. The brain connects with the world through the senses via nerve fibers and receives informative chemical signals. Then in some way not fully understood, consciousness emerges. A phenomenal representation of the world arises and the observer is represented in that presentation. The phenomenal representation is in the brain but we fail to appreciate this fact.

Some Thoughts on Consciousness

In social situations when people ask me what I'm doing I sometimes reveal that I'm working on a book about consciousness. Some people are excited by the topic and want to hear more, but others seem clearly uncomfortable with the subject. A few have said that their views on consciousness are tied to their religious beliefs, which are private and not open to question. To me, this lack of curiosity about consciousness is peculiar and could be a subject of research in itself. Perhaps the topic stirs up fear of the unknown by reminding people that there is little agreement about this and other profound matters; e.g. the extent of the universe, its age, its microscopic constituents, how we got here, life after death.

Beliefs concerning consciousness can be, sort of, divided into two headings:

1. Consciousness is something very different from matter
2. Consciousness and matter are not different.

1. Consciousness and Matter are Different

In these beliefs, often termed dualistic, consciousness can exist with or without matter. Mind/body, spirit/matter, soul/body are some of the more familiar terms used in this context. One of the major attractions of the dualistic belief is the possibility of something personal surviving the death of the body. Immortality! There are two main thoughts on this: one belief is that birth (or conception) is the beginning of an unending existence, the other belief holds that we have had previous life before birth (reincarnation). Both of these views agree that the next life may not necessarily be wonderful. The choices we make in this life affect the kind of afterlife we will have.[96]

Another dualistic ides envisions the existence of a field of consciousness, or a stream of consciousness, or a conscious energy with which we (our bodies) are in contact. At birth, the body connects up with this consciousness and personal experiences are recorded in the brain but with the passing of the body the personal stuff is lost but consciousness remains.

None of these belief systems offer any detailed explanation of consciousness and rather they take it as an unfathomable miracle. The reasons people give for accepting these beliefs are: tales of fragments of memory from previous lives, faith in a religious hierarchy or sacred document, the feeling that the belief must be true, personal spiritual experiences, tales of encounters with people who have died. Though no one of these offers much in the way of hard evidence the sheer number of such stories seem to be evidence enough for the people who hold such beliefs.[97]

2. Consciousness and Matter are not Different

In these beliefs, often termed monist, consciousness and matter are one. However, there are many variations on this "all is one" theme.[98]

1. Consciousness is the one thing that exists. Idealism.

2. Matter is the one thing. Materialism.

3. Some other stuff is the one, consciousness and matter are aspects of it; immaterialism, phenomenalism and others.

Idealism, in the extreme form, takes the position that our consciousness is all there is. In this view the material world is an assumption we incorrectly make in dealing with our phenomenal world. All is a dream. This view is particularly strong in Eastern thought, the term *Maya* refers to the illusory nature of the material world.

In Western thought the major thread is materialism. Matter is primary and exists independently of minds. Our mind, our consciousness, is a result of the organization and dynamic movement of matter. In this view, there is no consciousness without matter. An extreme form of materialism says only matter exists and seems to deny that we have mental states (consciousness), we only behave as if we were conscious.

The third monist view, with many variants (immaterialism, phenomenalism, hylozoism, panpsychism and others), contends that there is a physical world and that it, matter, is sentient or conscious. In this view rocks or molecules have some sort of internal knowing although it may be of a different quality from human consciousness.

Taking evolution seriously, we see each species is only a minute DNA step away from its predecessors. An unbroken chain of such steps links us all to primitive life forms. Where on this chain do we first find consciousness? Some people believe only humans are conscious because they alone possess a soul which, somehow, makes us conscious. I can't believe this. Anyone who has loved an animal (dog, cat, horse, chimp) has evidence for animal consciousness. But how var down the chain does consciousness go? Where does it emerge? Perhaps, it goes all the way down. Perhaps, like the qualities of matter (mass, charge, and spin), consciousness accompanies all bits of matter. David chalmer, in his book 'The Conscious Mind', is one of the more recent thinkers to discuss this possibility seriously.

The point of this brief and simple synopsis of world views is to give a glimpse into some of the many serious approaches to the question, what is existence? All these views acknowledge the importance of consciousness. I am totally ignoring any view that denies consciousness. Some say, "consciousness is all there is," others say, "there is consciousness and matter but they cannot be separated from each other," and finally others say, "conscious and matter both exist and can be separated from each other."

What comes next?

We are born into this world in a jumble of color, sound, smell, taste, touch, pleasure and pain...our phenomenal world. We notice certain regularly occurring sensations and rather quickly learn to interact with parents and the environment. By the age of one, many infants are learning to name things. By the age of two, the terrible twos, we begin to form a sense of self and other. If you know the story of Helen Keller, born both blind and deaf, you can appreciate the difficulty of developing these normal talents without the full range of senses. Most of us go on to accept our cultural bias (at least in the Western world) of an external material world. We acquire all sorts of cultural beliefs but it is the mark of a truly inquisitive person to transcend these generally accepted beliefs and see into something new.

Copernicus and Galileo saw into the fallacy of the immovable earth. Newton saw into the fallacy of heavenly versus earthly matter. Einstein challenged the constancy of matter and time. My bias is toward science and I don't know who to credit for discrediting; the Devine right of Kings, debtors prisons, inferiority of women, superiority of Caucasians, etc., but I am glad that these cultural assumptions have been brought to light. Raising our consciousness in these matters, so to speak.

In Physics we are still involved in uncovering the basic nature of matter. Particles or waves? Particles or wavy strings? How does observing matter influence it? How does quantum entanglement affect our world? It will take some time to answer these questions about matter but it seems clear that the answers will come, if they do come, through careful experiment and inspired thought.

The next revolution, I believe, will be a revolution in how our culture views consciousness. We have learned how hearts, livers, kidneys, lungs, intestines all function by the laws of physics....pressure, diffusion etc.. We seem to be machines, biological machines. In fact, all of these organs just mentioned and others have been transplanted from one person to another without changing the consciousness of the recipient. Even very small injuries to the brain can cause noticable changes in consciousness. The brain seems to be the biological unit that produces consciousness. However we don't know how the brain does what it does. The brain has been mapped to a great extent, and we have a pretty good understanding of the function of various parts of the brain although we don't know the details of how the various functions are accomplished. For example, language and thought have been linked to certain areas in the left hemisphere (of most people) and damage to those areas leads to loss of those functions but does not affect the consciousness[99] or the emotions of the person. Alzheimer's patients suffer a similar loss of speech and thought but remain conscious, although their consciousness might be severely impaired.

Like the other apes, we are animals. We came from animals. Consciousness, most likely, is a biological function...like digestion and reproduction. Consciousness in lower animals, say worms, or in plants would have to be very different from human consciousness, if there is any consciousness at all, because of the lack of a developed nervous system.

How does the brain produce consciousness? Of course, no one knows. The most popular approach right now is to implicate the many neurons of the brain in some sort of orchestrated activity, which then causes us to be conscious. The suggestion is that groups or layers of neurons receive input (nerve signals) from higher and lower layers and in turn produce output to those and other layers. Brain workers are trying to uncover the elaborate mapping of communication between neurons in the brain. But there is no compelling explanation as to how all this activity would produce, for example, the visual and auditory experiences we have when awake or when dreaming.

Others suggest that neurons, though numerous, are too coarse to be the ultimate source of consciousness. They look for much smaller structures within brain cells on which to pin their hopes. Hameroff and Penrose hope that microtubles threading through our cells might provide the necessary environment for quantum mechanical effects to be supported in brains. This reminds me of the emergence of superconductivity in certain materials. The metal lead, ordinarily a poor conductor of electricity, if cooled to within a few degrees of absolute zero undergoes a remarkable transition. Although the atomic structure does not change, the electrons within the metal somehow pair up and then can effortlessly dance around the metal atoms without losing energy. A current established in a ring of metal, if kept cold, can persist unassisted for years. This superconductivity is a quantum effect and is an emergent phenomenon. Other materials have been discovered that can do the same thing but at much higher temperatures. The record now is a copper perovskite, which needs to be cooled to a mere -135 degrees Celsius (-211 Fahrenheit). A dream of these workers is to achieve room temperature superconductivity. Perhaps the microtubles of the brain produce some organic room temperature quantum states, which are our conscious states. But still there is no way that even this situation gives any explanation of the reds and blues of our experience.

No one has any ideas on how physical matter, organic or inorganic, can produce the qualities we experience in our phenomenal presentation...the colors, sounds, tastes etc. This leads many to take the position that it will always remain an unfathomable mystery. The "explanatory gap" is too wide. This is the "hard problem." They feel we will never bridge the worlds of reality and phenomena.

This leads others to consider more radical suggestions. Perhaps matter is conscious. A crystal of quartz might have some kind of private, internal experience as the warmth of your fingers warms up one end of it. A crystal is an ordered array of atoms held together by a sea of electrons flooding the array. The atoms and electrons are governed by quantum principles and the whole thing is a complex quantum state. The warmth of your touch will slightly increase the inter atomic distances in the vicinity of the touch and alter the quantum state in some way. Perhaps this quantum state might endow the crystal with an awareness of it surroundings. Even an atom, with its nucleus and electrons is a quantum object and might have a very rudimentary awareness, and when combined into a molecule where some electrons can move over the entire unit then a more rich awareness occurs. When molecules combine in ordered arrays, crystals, more interesting internal states ensue. Perhaps it is like something to be a crystal, in the same sense that it is like something to be a human being or like something to be a bat. The suggestion is that humans, bats and crystals have some sort of consciousness that goes along with them.

In this view, matter does not cause consciousness, which seems to require an explanation, but rather, matter is conscious. Of course it is obvious that such a view is untestable. We could never do any test to convince ourselves that a crystal is conscious in some way. Although in fairness to those who hold such a view, I must admit that there is no test that I could perform to convince myself that other people are conscious. My belief that other people are conscious does not come from tests. If someone constructed a lifelike robot no test could prove or disprove its possessing consciousness. So holding the belief that matter is conscious, or believing that matter is not conscious, is not provable or disprovable. It is a sort of religious belief that is beyond the realm of science. Animism, the belief that all matter is alive or has consciousness, has been around for millennia and is still around today.

John Searle[100] dismisses the suggestion of universal consciousness, panpsychism as absurd, with no further discussion, but perhaps he is too quick here. If elementary units of matter do have some internal sensations does this have any possible consequence? Darwin's theory of natural selection, the so called survival of the fittest, is an attempt to explain how we have arisen from simpler ancestors. We survive because we have changed to be better at surviving. To some this seems like an empty truism with no explanatory power, like saying, this creature has survived because it is better at survival. Of course Darwin says the changes are random, some good, some bad, and competition makes the selection of who survives. But, in the spirit of inquiry, what if changes are driven by some tendency to increase consciousness...which as a by-product increases the survival rate. What if consciousness is useful in survival. The creature with superior consciousness is superior at surviving. (We must keep in mind that some very simple creatures, perhaps without any consciousness, have survived for billions of years and must be classed as very successful.)The opponents to Darwin, the Intelligent Design group, can't accept that blind matter, even over an enormous span of time, can come to what it has come to. Matter needs help they say. Perhaps consciousness provides that help. I am conscious, I assume you too are conscious and maybe all matter is conscious. We are more conscious than vermin or virus but we share that important property...consciousness. The preceding is my attempt to share the mind of the panpsychists. I don't go so far as saying I accept these beliefs but when you are at an intellectual dead end, a little uncritical brainstorming can't hurt.

While brainstorming, we should keep in mind that our current understanding of matter is much different from that held in the early 1900's. Our concept of matter is undergoing radical changes. Here are four of the most challenging discoveries.

1. "Earthly matter" is intermingled with four times as much "dark matter." This other kind of matter, dark matter, is a postulated substance, completely transparent to light and all electromagnetic radiations but it still apparently interacts with ordinary matter (earth, stars, galaxies) through gravity. The evidence: Observation of rotation of galaxies. Galaxies do not rotate like a whirlpool or tornado but like a huge wheel. The observed mass of the galaxy, its stars, dust, gas, planets, moons etc., is not enough to hold the galaxy together. It needs four times as much matter to account for its self gravitation. But this extra matter cannot be detected by our telescopes, radio receivers, absorption studies...hence the term "dark matter." Also there is evidence from the ability of gravity to bend light. Large lumps of dark matter can act as a gravitational lens and distort the images of visible matter behind them by bending the light that passes through them.

2. Recently "dark energy" is currently thought to be about three times as abundant as "dark matter," i.e. dark energy 75%, dark matter 20% and regular matter 5%. The evidence: Analyzing the distribution of certain types of bright stellar explosions. Astronomers have techniques by which they can assign a distance and speed to these cosmic events. These assignments lead to the conclusion that the expansion of the universe is not slowing down but is speeding up. Dark energy is the term for the hypothetical energy providing the ongoing push of this expansion. This energy, like dark matter, is invisible to our instruments but acts to provide the pressure driving the accelerating expansion. The mysterious dark matter/energy is 20 times more abundant than known matter.

3. Small bits of matter(electrons, atoms, small molecules) and light (photons) have been caused to interacted in a special way as to remain in touch with each other over many meters. This connection is called entanglement(or quantum entanglement or quantanglement). This is a fundamental

property of matter predicted by quantum mechanics. For a pair of entangled particles, measuring the spin of one particle immediately ensures that measuring the spin of its partner will reveal the opposite value of spin. If this spin correlation were caused by a signal it would have to have a speed much faster than that of light. This entanglement has been demonstrated over large distances and it is assumed that it holds even for enormous distances. Light emitted from a galaxy far far away is still entangled with photons we can collect tonight.

4. Matter and energy, when on the move, take all possible paths at once. The particles of matter do not have values for their speed and position until, by interacting with them, the values are, shall we say, selected from the spectrum of possible values. This gives matter a certain wave like behavior. Using entanglement and the wave nature of matter people are building quantum computers that can perform all possible computations simultaneously.[101]

My point is, we are still learning about the properties of matter. Not in some expected way, like finding element number 121, but in unexpected ways. Unexpected like the discovery of; superconductivity (when matter is made extremely cold), laser action, quantum entanglement, dark matter, dark energy...these were all unsuspected and surprising. Matter isn't the simple stuff we used to think it was. We don't know how consciousness is connected to matter but we don't fully understand matter. So it may be premature to reject the idea that matter might be conscious.

Appendix

II

Stop me if you've heard this. That is, the information in this section is well known and can be found in most physiology texts. But if somehow you have missed it, then this will be very interesting.

Most people seem to know that the higher brain is divided into two halves, the left and right hemisphere, connected by a thick bundle of nerves, the corpus callosum. How this is better than an undivided brain is not known, but it is clearly evident when injury to the right brain causes motor malfunctions in the left side of the body and vice versa. A stroke in the left brain will in most cases affect the ability to speak and cause trouble on the right side of the body. Even if we could come up with some reason as to why splitting the brain would be advantageous there seems to be no explanation as to why this crossover. Wouldn't it be simpler for the left brain to control the left side of the body and the right brain the right side?

What is less generally known but more relevant to our investigations is that this left/right splitting and crossover is evident in the visual system. The retina, which is the light-sensitive covering on the back of each eyeball, is also split into left and right halves. Not the retina really but the bundle of nerves connected to the left side of the retina, crosses over and informs the visual layers of the right brain and vice versa. When you are looking at a scene in front of you, the eye system sends the left half of the scene to the right hemisphere of the brain and the right half of the scene to the left hemisphere. Then, with the aid of the connecting corpus callosum the two halves are fused into one seamless presentation. What a strange way to do business.

Interesting things can be revealed by testing people whose corpus callosum has been cut. (This has sometimes been done surgically to relieve severe epilepsy.) When such subjects are presented with objects in their left visual field, information that goes to their right hemisphere, they are unable to talk about the objects (talking being a left hemisphere function). However they can select a similar object by feel from a bag using their left hand (which is controlled by the right hemisphere).

Also there are those cases of hemispheric neglect. People who have brain lesions in the right side of their brain will sometimes "lose sight of" objects in the left side of their visual field. The may only eat the food on the left side of their plate. They seem unaware of the left side and are also unaware of this deficit in their abilities.

Knowing from physiology that the visual scene we are presented with is a fusion of the work of our left and right hemispheres, yet it does not seem evident when we inspect the scene before us (within us). It is seamless, left and right join perfectly. The scene is so good it seems real.

Appendix

III

What follows is a short article written for the publication *The Link* which can be accessed at KLI@kmail.ch

"Is no one inspired by our present picture of the universe? Our poets do not write about it; our artists do not try to portray this remarkable thing. The value of science remains unsung by singers: you are reduced to hearing not a song or poem, but an evening lecture about it. This is not yet a scientific age." Richard Feynman

This piece is a defense of materialism, which is often put in opposition to spiritualism and dualism. Does matter need help from spirit to provide understanding to all we encounter in life? I believe that science is a long way from understanding matter but as more is learned more seemingly mysterious phenomena are understood. To keep things lighthearted, I present an imagined dialog between Matt, a materialist, and Spiro, an open minded spiritualist (or dualist).

Spiro: Why, Matt, do you believe the brain is so important for consciousness.

Matt: The brain is the organ of consciousness. Injury to the liver, or lungs, or legs does not affect consciousness but even slight bumps to the head can do damage to the way we perceive the world. Minute quantities of certain chemicals have tremendous impact on consciousness. Can you go along with that?

Spiro: Yes, but I feel that there must be something more than the brain to account for the richness of consciousness. The soul connects to the matter of the body, through the brain, and gives it life.

Matt: We don't need the soul to handle digestion or respiration or procreation do we? What special function does the soul perform?

Spiro: What about consciousness or love?

Matt: People have talked about love for millennia and have not come to a satisfactory conclusion. The word "love" is difficult to define and leads to ineffable solutions. If you don't mind I'll stick to consciousness—that which you see, hear, feel, taste, and smell. Our brains connect to the world outside the body through the sense organs. The eyes, for example, focus light on the cells of the retina which, through nerve fibers of the optic tract, send a chemical/electrical signal to the visual part of the brain. In similar fashion, the ears have tiny hairs to detect various vibrations in the air and convert the movement to similar signals going to the auditory part of the brain.

Spiro: Yes, all that is well known. Each of the senses send similar signals to brain areas.

Matt: If one of the sensory pathways or the corresponding brains area is damaged, there is a loss of that function. Damage to the optic path results in blindness. Lesions in only a portion of the visual area lead to loss of vision in part of the visual field.

Spiro: What's your point in all this?

Matt: The point is we, that is our brains, do not have immediate contact with the world outside the body. The connection to the world is mediated by the nerves. The brain has inherited, from previous life forms over millions of years, the ability to read nerve signals and construct an internal brainscape which presents the brain's best attempt at modeling the world outside. Each of us has lived with this brainscape since birth—it is all we know. We mistake the brainscape for a real world, but it is not the real world—it is a virtual reality, like a 3-D video game.

Spiro: I read that the brain makes an image which it projects outside of the body.

Matt: In addition to the senses already mentioned, the brain collects information on the status of the body. It can sense heat, cold, pain, the angle of the joints, the rotation of the eyes, and other subtle body facts. From these data, along with what the eyes can see of the body, the brain constructs an image of its body which is included in the brainscape. When we look around our virtual reality we see and feel our body at the center of it.

Spiro: This is rather startling. This brainscape is somewhat like a dream.

Matt: That's right. Dreams show us we have the brain-power to generate very convincing images. I'm sure you understand that color is not in the electro-magnetic energy which reaches the eyes, and that there is no sound in air-pressure variations touching the ears—color and sound are the brain's creations. So try this; look straight ahead and gently press on the side of one eyeball. Now you see two worlds in front of you. Obviously they can't both be real and the fact is neither is real—both are virtual brain creations. Or this; hold a finger before your eyes and focus on it but attend to the images beyond it. Do they appear double to you?

Spiro: Well, yes they do. But I see now that I don't need the finger, I can focus at any distance and the world beyond, as well as the nearer world, appears double—I just never noticed it before doing this simple exercise. This reminds me of Plato's famous parable of the cave where he asks us to consider a prisoner constrained to view only the back wall of a cave where shadows of people and things are cast by a fire outside. Since this is all the prisoner has ever seen he mistakes it for reality.

Matt: Exactly. Plato learned this from Socrates who was using the fire-shadow analogy to get his point across. Today we could update the parable to consider a person who, from birth, is wearing a virtual reality helmet which enables each eye to see a slightly different image and thus to sense a 3-D virtual experience—with color and sound.

Spiro: But wait! If the world and by body image are virtual, then what is going on inside my head? I can see the edges of my eye sockets, part of my nose and lips, and can feel the back of my but if all this is virtual, what is going on inside of this virtual head?

Matt: Nothing is happening in the head you partially display in your brainscape. It is more correct to say, the virtual head is happening in the brain—along with thought. Thought is happening in your head but not in the virtual image of your head. We are mistaken if we imagine ourselves to operate behind our eyes. We are operating all over the brainscape.

Spiro: Wow! Too much at once. How do materialists explain the brain's ability to create consciousness?

Matt: There is no explanation. It is still a big mystery. Some think consciousness emerges from complex connection in neural networks. Others favor quantum mechanical effects within brain cells. My current favorite is complex electro-magnetic fields associated with neural activity. Others suggest that matter has conscious qualities yet to be discovered.

Spiro: You are saying it is a mystery. We live in our virtual brainscape and whatever is outside of us is also a mystery.

Matt: Yes, that's right. The scientific study of matter and consciousness is still in its infancy. Photons, quarks, strings, multiple universes, the big-bang are our best guesses as to what is out there. The tip of the iceberg.

Spiro: What about people who have had mystical experiences?

Matt: For me, realizing the world I once thought was real is a virtual world occurring in my brain, was a mystical experience. I guess many people have similar glimpses of this and are similarly mystified.

Spiro: I think I get your point. I have always felt that mere matter was lacking life. But you are offering me a view of consciousness which is quite spiritual. Consciousness, as we experience it, is filled with colors, and music, and flavors, and odors, and sensations which are not material, but, to me, kind of spiritual. This merits looking into.

Spiro: How do you handle the question of life after death?

Matt: Why do you even think there is a life continuing after the death of the body?

Spiro: Well all those stories about ghosts and also everybody I know seems to just accept the notion. Certainly, it makes me feel better to think that death is not the end. I have many friends who feel that that have lived before——-passed lives, and all that.

Matt: I have heard all those stories, too. I have come to regard them as artifacts of previous cultures, still having a great influence on the culture of the present. Many different threads of thought persist on the earth today. I strongly feel that we must examine our beliefs and try to understand from whence they came. I was strongly influenced by a Christian background but began to see problems with that way of thought when I reached the age of reason.

Spiro: Some people I know feel that thought probably is material, but that there is something other, something that is not material which may choicelessly enter awareness—call it insight. What do you think of that?

Matt: I feel uncomfortable with this question. It leaves me wondering if I even understand the question. I have had occasions which I would call insight, but would these people you know agree that these occasions were the insight of which they speak? In my case, I think my brain, after much unconscious churning, caused a dramatic change in my consciousness. I would be overreaching if I suggested this was evidence for non-material activity.

Thus, Spiro and Matt end their dialog before they get too agitated. I apologize for giving Matt most of the best lines, but I hope he was not insulting. If you want to comment on this article my email address is: zorskie@gmail.com

Bibliography

Audi, Robert: editor (1995) *The Cambridge Dictionary of Philosophy* Cambridge: Cambridge University Press

Ayer, Alfred J. (1940) *The Foundations of Empirical Knowledge* New York: MacMillan & Co Ltd

Baars, Bernard J., Gage, Nicole M. (2007) *Cognition, Brain, and Consciousness* New York: Elsevier

Blackburn, Simon: (1994) *Oxford Dictioinary of Philosophy* Oxford: Oxford University Press

306

Blackmore, Susan (2006) *Conversations on Consciousness* Oxford: Oxford University Press

Carruthers, Peter (2005) *Consciousness; Essays from a Higher-Order Perspective* Oxford: Clarendon Press

Chalmers, David J. (1996) *The Conscious Mind* New York: Oxford University Press

Churchland, P. M. (2007) *Neurophilosophy at Work* Cambridge: Cambridge University Press.

Crick, Francis (1994) *The Astonishing Hypothesis*

Dahlbom, Bo, (1993) *Dennett and His Critics* Oxford: Blackwell

Damasio, Antonio (1999) *The Feeling of What Happens* New York: Harvest Books

Damasio, Antonio (2003) *Looking for Spinoza* New York: Harvest Books

Davies, Paul (2007) *Cosmic Jackpot* Houghton Mifflin Company, Boston, New York

Dawkins, Richard ( ) *The Selfish Gene*

Dawkins, Richard (2006) *The God Delusion* New York: Houghton Mifflin Company

Deacon, Terrence W. (1997) *The Symbolic Species* New York: W. W. Norton & Company

Dennett, Daniel C. (1991) *Consciousness Explained* New York: Penguin Books

Dennett, Daniel C. (1995) *Darwin's Dangerous Idea* New York: Simon & Schuster Paperbacks

Dennett, Daniel C. (1996) *Kinds of Minds* New York: Basic Books

Dennett, Daniel C. (2003) *Freedom Evolves* New York: Viking Press

Dennett, Daniel C. (2006) *Breaking the Spell* New York: Viking Press

308

Edelman, Gerald M. (2004) *Wider Than the Sky* New Haven: Yale University Press

Gazzaniga, Michael S. *(1985) The Social Brain: Discovering the Networks of the Mind*

Gazzaniga, Michael S. *(1989) Mind Matters*

Gazzaniga, Michael S. *(1994) Nature's Mind*

Gazzaniga, Michael S. *(2005) The Mind's Past*

Gazzaniga, Michael S. *(2005) The Ethical Brain* New York: Harper Perennial

Goswami, Amit. (1993) *The Self Aware Universe* New York: Tarcher/Penguin

Gregory, Richard (1966) *Eye and Brain* Hawkins, Jeff (2004) *On Intelligence* New York: Henry Holt and Company

Hobson, J. Allan (1988) *The Dreaming Brain:* New York: Basic Books

Hofstadter, Douglas R. (1979) *Godel, Escher, Bach:* New York: Vintage Books

Hofstadter, Douglas R. (2007) *I Am A Strange Loop:* New York: Basic Books

Hofstadter, Douglas R., Dennett, Daniel (1981) *The Mind's I:* New York: Bantam Books

James, William., (1956) *The Will To Believe*: New York: Dover Publications (first printing 1897)

Kafatos, Menas., Nadeau, Robert. (1990) *The Conscious Universe* New York: Springer-Verlag

Kandel, Eric R. (2006) *In Search of Memory* New York: W. W. Norton & Company

LaBerge, Stephen. (2004) *Lucid Dreaming* Boulder, CO: Sounds True. Inc.

Laughlin, Robert B. (2005) *A Different Universe* New York: Basic Books

Lehrer, Jonah (2007) *Proust was a Neuroscientist* New York: Houghton Mifflin Company

Lockwood, Michael. (1989) *Mind, Brain and the Quantum* Great Britain: Athenaeum Press

McCrone, John (1999) *Going Inside* New York: Fromm International

McGinn, Colin (1989) Can we solve the mind-body problem? *Mind*
98: 349-366

McGinn, Colin (1999) *The Mysterious Flame* New York: Basic Books

McGinn, Colin (1999) *The Making of a Philosopher* New York: Perennial Books

Metzinger, T. (2000) Introduction: Consciousness research at the end of the twentieth century. In T. Metzinger, ed. *Neural Correlates of Consciousness—Empirical and Conceptual Questions.* Cambridge, MA: MIT Press

Metzinger, T. (2004) *Being No One. The Self-Model Theory of Subjectivity.* Cambridge, MA: MIT Press.

Metzinger, T. (2009) *The Ego Tunnel* New York: Basic Books

Nagel, Thomas (1997) *The Last Word* Oxford: Oxford University Press

Nagel, Thomas (1986) *The View From Nowhere* Oxford: Oxford University Press

Ornstein, Robert. (1997) *The Right Mind* New York: Harcourt Brace

Penrose, Roger, with Abner Shimony, Nancy Cartwright and Stephan Hawking (1997) *The Large, the Small and the Human Mind* Cambridge: Cambridge University Press.

Penrose, Roger (1989) *The Emperor's New Mind* New York: Oxford University Press

Penrose, Roger (1994) *Shadows of the Mind* New York: Oxford University Press

312

Restak, Richard (1995) *Brainscapes* New York: Hyperion

Ramachandran, V. S., Blakeslee, Sandra., Sacks, Oliver. (1999) *Phantoms in the Brain*

Ramachandran, V. S. (2005) *A Brief Tour of Human Consciousness* New York, Pi Press

Revonsuo, Antti, (2006) *Inner Presence* Cambridge, Massachusetts, The MIT Press

Rosenfield, Israel (1992) *The Strange, Familiar and Forgotten* New York: Alfred A. Knopf

Sartre, Jean-Paul (1964) *Nausea* New York: New Directions Publishing Company

Schrodinger, E. (1944) *What is Life?* Cambridge: Cambridge University Press.

Searle, John R. (2004) *Mind: a brief introduction* Oxford: Oxford University Press

Searle, John R. (1997) *The Mystery of Consciousness* New York: New York Review

Wegner, Daniel M., (2002) *The Illusion of Conscious Will* Cambridge, MA, The MIT Press

Zeman, Adam, (2002) *Consciousness* New Haven and London: Yale University Press

Endnotes

1   This is actually the Latin translation of the Greek inscription, *gnothi seauton*.

2   Perhaps Socrates would agree to rephrasing his famous line as: Only the examined life is worth living. Daniel Dennett would then ask–worth it to whom? Cui bono? (See his book *Freedom Evolves*.) Who benefits when a person lives an examined life? What is the benefit? This is an important topic, but it is relegated to this note because we will discuss it in the last chapter. It would be a mistake to delay embarking on the examination by insisting on identifying the benefit.

3 The tale, also called the "Parable of the Cave", is in book VII of Plato's *Republic*. There are many translations but they are all quite similar. The version in the following paragraphs comes from the website: http://classics.mit.edu/Plato/republic.html

4 See page 314, Ray Kurzweil, *The Singularity Is Near*, 2005

5 Nicolas Copernicus, *De revolutionibus orbium coelestium* (*On the Revolutions of the Heavenly Spheres*) Amherst, Prometheus Books, 1995, p. 8. Originally published in Nuremberg, 1543. This quote and reference is taken from Paul Davies' book, *Cosmic Jackpot*, p. 129.

6 The word was later translated into Latin by Cicero. See page 332 of the book *Cognition, Brain, and Consciousness* by Baars and Gage.

7 I first encountered this remark in the writings of J. Krishnamurti. It has almost become his trademark quotation. It is not clear to me if he was using it in the way that WYSIRY is intended.

8 For example, Metzinger in *Being No One*, p. 152.

9   Russell, B. *Human Knowledge: Its Scope and Limits*. London: George Allen and Unwin LTD. (1948).

10 For an excellent exposure to brain research see J. Allen Hobson's *The Dreaming Brain* (1989)

11 Godwin, Malcolm, 1994, *The Lucid Dreamer, A Waking Guide for the Traveler Between Worlds, New York,* Simon & Schuster.

12 For dreams: see J. Allen Hobson's *The Dreaming Brain* (1989)

13 TMS was given a huge boost by an engineering group at the University of Sheffield in 1985. In 1988 a group at Cadwell Laboratories started using repetitive pulses, rTMS, in the 1 to 50 hertz range.

14 I was schooled as a physicist, so please excuse my indulgence in these explanations.

15 Redrawn from Siegal, R. K. 1977 "Hallucinations", *Scientific American*. 273, 132—140.

16 Redrawn from Clottes, J. and Lewis-Williams, D. 1998 *The Shamans of Prehis-*

tory: Trance and Magic in the Painted Caves, New York: Abrams.

17 The retina is peculiar in that it is somewhat "inside out." In the octopus, light passes through the lens and then hits a layer of photoreceptors that connect to optic nerves that go to the brain. In humans, the retina's photoreceptors are not in the first layers that light encounters. They are behind a layer of cells that give rise to the optic nerve. The light must pass through this layer to get to the rods and cones and the optic nerve must pass through the rod/cone layer to get to the brain. The spot where the optic nerve passes is insensitive to light. It seems like a case of poor design.

18 At this point I resist the temptation to say that the brain *fills in* the area of the blind spot to match the surrounding area. I am hesitant because I remember Daniel Dennett's objection (p. 344 of Consciousness Explained): "This idea of *filling in* is common in the thinking of even sophisticated theorists, and it is a dead giveaway of vestigial Cartesian

materialism. What is amusing is that those who use the term often know better, but since they find the term irresistible, they cover themselves by putting it in scare-quotes. For instance, just about everyone describes the brain as 'filling in' the blind spot..." He goes on to give a very long explanation of why the term should not be used.

19 See pages 90-97 in *Phantoms in the Brain* by Ramachandran and Blakeslee.

20 Redrawn from Tyler, C. W. 1978 "Some new entopic phenomena." *Vision Research.* 181.

21 In an article called "Shielding Space Travelers," (*Scientific American*, March 2006) points out that in a spacecraft about 5,000 cosmic rays (mostly high energy protons) pass through the body each second. In one year about a third of the astronaut's DNA would be cut. It would take five meters of water to shield against such particles.

22 See "The Mind: Biological Approaches to its Functions" Editors: William C.

Corning, Martin Balaban, 1968, pp. 233—258.

23 In his book *The Feeling of What Happens.*

24 Because the earth is turning on its axis the shadow will move toward the east. A stick alined with the two stones is quite close to east-west. You can use this anywhere on earth to get your bearings.

25 To reduce flicker, each frame is projected three times. We see 72 frames each second but only 24 different frames.

26 In fluorescent tubes, a current of electrons passes through a gas and causes it to emit light. Some of the emitted light is not in our visible range so a coating is put on the tube to absorb that light and emit the energy as visible light.

27 My friend is Donn Gladstone. Together with John Hidley we have created a website based on the ideas of this book, www.museumofconsciousness. com . Our hope is to interest people into actually building a museum devoted to consciousness.

28 Donn Gladstone (private communication) points out that 3-D as we see it should be called maybe 2.1-D. When we look at an object we see only the facet of it that faces us; in true 3-D we would see all sides of the object.

29 Julez, B. "Binocular Depth Perception of Computer Generated Patterns. Bell Systems Technical Journals 39, 1125—162.

30 http://brahms.cpmc.colombia.edu/publications/stereo-review.pdf

31 Our two eyes, three inches apart, provide two points of view that enable us to reconstruct the locations and volumes of objects within 30 feet of us. Birds have two eyes but they are much closer together than our eyes. I have noticed birds bobbing their heads up and down and I suspect that this enhances their depth perception by increasing the separation of their points of view.

32 http://cns-alumni.bu.edu/~slehar/Lehar.html

33 h t t p : / / w w w . p s y . r i t s u m e i . ac.jp/~akitaoka/index-e.html. This site has hundreds of illusions. Browse through and marvel at the tricks our visual system can play on us.

34 See Churchland's *Neurophilosophy at Work*, around page 186.

35 I don't know the name of this effect, but I'd bet it has a name. Since I got interested in illusions a few decades ago, I have learned many little tricks that I thought were original discoveries, and since then I have found practically all of them in print. Some of them have been known for centuries, and a person comes across them mostly by chance.

36 Many classic illusions, including some with animation, can be viewed on the website http://www.questacon.edu.au/html/illusions_teacher_materials.html.

37 Lasers usually emit their energy in several almost parallel directions causing the output to look non-uniform. If the output is passed into a lens, each different direction will focus to a different

spot. Placing a screen with a single pinhole in that focal plane will allow only a single mode to pass. This is a simple way to clean up the output of a laser.

38 Laser light, unlike that from a flashlight, is coherent. This allows different sections of the output to add or subtract when they are combined. The light falling on any particular retinal cell is a combination of various photons reflected off the viewing screen. This total summation can be bright or dark depending on the position of the cell with respect to the screen, leading to an overall grainy pattern of received energy on the retina.

39 Metzinger (in *Being No One*) writes about colors we can discriminate and those we can recognize. We are ten times better at seeing the difference in colors presented side by side than we are at recognizing their difference when presented singly. We are even worse at naming them. We can easily name yellow and green and even yellow-green but yellow-yellow-green or green-yellow-green are much more

difficult. Perhaps we can discriminate 50 "reds." Red32 looks different next to red33 but shown singly they appear to be the same.

40 http://www.mercola.com/images/ newsletter/2005/06/28/illusion.gif

41 I read the word "moire" comes from weavers who use "mohair"

42 You can see Moire` patterns in highway overpasses with fences on both sides of the structure, a screen and its shadow, reflections of single screens, fencing around property. Once while driving I thought I saw a shape approaching from the side but it turned out to be a shifting Moire` pattern generated by parallel fences.

43 The exhibit, in New York City, was entitled E A T. It was a collaboration between artists and technologists. There was another striking contribution: two eight foot concave mirrors faced each other with a corridor between them. When you entered the space you saw a life-sized reflection of yourself, but unlike with flat mirrors, the image was in front of the mirrors (in the space with

you). When you put out your right hand, the image put out its right hand. I tried to shake hands with my image, but as the two hands approached, the image of the hand faded. It was a memorable illusion.

44 As a graduate student, in the mid-1960s, I made a few holograms with a pulsed ruby laser and with a HeNe laser (using an inner tube for vibration damping).

45 The website http://www.livescience.com/scienceoffiction/050927_virtusphere.html contains a description of a spherical cage that the user can walk within while wearing a VR helmet. Walking rotates the cage and changes the display in the helmet to give the impression of strolling through an alternate reality.

46 At a 3-D show in Las Vegas there was a virtual roller coaster first going up then plunging down. Even though the theater chair was not moving, I got a feeling in my gut of falling. I never liked that sensation and always thought it was a reaction to falling, but I now realize that I generate that feeling.

47   Botvinick M., Cohen J. Rubber hands "feel" touch that eyes see. *Nature* 1988:391.756.

48   This is from a paper presented at the 2007 meeting of the Association for the Scientific Study of Consciousness. "The Experimental Induction of Out-of-Body Experience." Presented by H. Henrik Ehrsson of the Karolinska Institute, Stockholm, Sweden.

49   Attributed to V. S. Ramachandran.

50   Waist shrinking illusion. Ehrsson, H. H.; Kito, T.; Passingham, R. E.; Naito, E.; *PloS Biol* Dec. 2005 3(12):e412.

51   *Scientific American* Nov. 2005

52   V. S. Ramachandran, *A Brief Tour of Human Consciousness*, 2004, Pi Press, New York, p. 12.

53   I was pleased to have stumbled on this illusion by myself, and only recently found that Aristotle had used it more than 2000 years ago.

54   Sampio, E., Maris, S., Bach-y-Rita, P. 2001 "Brain Plasticity": Visual Acuity of Blind Persons Via the Tongue. Brain Research 908(July 13):204. Many websites describe the research, including that of

a company formed to market the device, www.wicab.com.

55 This is not really relevant, but David Bohm liked to point out that the past tense of thinking is thought, and the past tense of feeling is felt (here feeling includes the emotions). So we are often driven by our thoughts and felts. The feeling is over but the felt remains.

56 See page 221 of P. Churchland's *Neurophilosophy at Work*.

57 This coin trick comes from an article by the Ramachandrans in April/May 2006 *Scientific American Mind*.

58 Geldard FA, Sherrick CE, "The Cutaneous 'Rabbit': a Perceptual Illusion". *Science*(1972) vol. 178, issue 4057, pp. 178—179.

59 The speed of sound in air is roughly 1000 feet per second, which is about one-milisecond per foot (the distance between ears is about a foot). This speed is also about 1/5 mile per second, so if you see a flash of lightning and 10 seconds later you hear thunder, then the strike is two miles away.

60 Nagel, T. 1974. "What Is It Like to Be a Bat"? *Philosophical Review* 4:435-50.

61 I can't resist pointing out that the word "inform" comes from "in" and "form," a recognition that information changes something within us.

62 Matthew Kelly of the National Institute on Deafness and Other Communication Disorders is hopeful that transplanting hair cells from the vestibular system into the cochlear area will restore hearing in certain types of deafness.

63 Umami is said to be found in the flavor of asparagus, tomatoes, cheese, meat, soy sauce, and miso. Professor Kikunea Ikeda isolated the flavor and determined it was glutamic acid, from which he created monosodium glutamate, MSG.

64 I recall also that the next morning some broccoli growers dumped tons of broccoli on his front lawn.

65 One is 6-n-propylthiouracil (PROP) mentioned in an article by Stefanie Reinberger in *Scientific American Mind* June/July 2006 ,"Bitter Could Be Better."

66 The amygdala has direct access to the olfactory bulb.

67 The prevalent theory of smell is similar to the lock and key theory of taste. However, recently a theory of molecular vibration has been proposed. Turin, Lucas (1996) "A Spectroscopic Mechanism for Primary Olfactory Reaction", *Chemical Senses.* 21(6):773-791 suggests that our noses may be sensitive to infrared vibrations of molecules. Chemicals with different isotopes in the chemical structure have the same shape (key) but have different molecular vibrations due to the different mass of the components.

68 Gordon M. Shepard, "Smell Images and Flavor System in the Human Brain." *Nature* 444, 316—321 (16 Nov 2006) Insight.

69 There is an organ, the vomeronasal organ (VNO) in the nasal cavity, which many think is the detecting system for pheromones, but no nerves have been found that connect it to the brain. No indisputable proof for human phero-

mones has been published in peer-reviewed articles.

70 Recently a forth type of photodetector has been found in the retinas of humans. In addition to rods and cones, David Berson has discovered that certain ganglion cells are sensitive to (blue) light and are involved in setting our circadian rhythms. Berson, D. M. (2003) "Strange Vision: Ganglion Cells as Circadian Photoreceptors". *Trends in Neuroscience* 26:314-320.

71 See the article by R. Douglas Fields, "The Shark's Electric Sense'", *Scientific American*, August 2007.

72 Phenomena such as Kirlian photography and seeing auras surrounding people are sometimes mentioned along with electric field sensing, but I judge that simpler explanations for these effects are probable.

73 While searching for "magnetic sense" on the web I encountered a site reporting that Todd Huffman had a small silicone-coated neodymium magnet implanted in a finger. He says, "I am now able to perceive magnetic fields

in ways not naturally possible." He claims to sense the fields of theft detection devices in store doorways, and the magnetic effects of small electric motors.

74 My wife is excellent with color, which shows in her watercolors. You can see them at her website sharonrussellart.com.

75 The nuclear force is now better understood as an aspect of quark interactions. The electromagnetic force is now understood to include the weak force. Some physicists like David Bohm and Basil Hiley, try to consider quantum mechanical effects as a fourth force, the quantum potential, acting on the particles of nature.

76 John McCrone's book *Going Inside: A Tour Round a Single Moment of Consciousness* (1999), does an extraordinary job unfolding what we know happens in the brain during the fraction of a second between stimulus and experience.

77 This quote and the preceding one are on pages 146 and 147 of McCrone's *Going Inside*.

78 In 1999, Amadou Diallo was killed by police as he offered his wallet. See Cordelia Fine, *A Mind of Its Own: How Your Brain Distorts and Deceives*, for this and other instances of how the conscious experience is shaped by the unconscious.

79 An article in *Scientific American*, June 2006, "The Implicit Prejudice", about the work of Harvard psychologist Mahzarin Banaji tells of a similar video where a basketball game has a woman with a white umbrella walk across the scene. This is part of her work on implicit association testing (IAT).

80 Much of the work on "blindsight" is due to Weiskrantz, L., Sanders, M. D. & Marshall, J. (1974) "Visual capacity in the hemianopic field following a restricted cortical ablation", Brain 97:709-28. Much of that work is based on patient GY who, after much additional work, is now said to experience some sort of visual percept in his blind field.

81 See Damasio, *The Feeling of What Happens.*

82 See *Scientific American,* December 2005.

83 Of course, air is always present in our experience yet we do not experience it as part of us. Vision is only one of the sensations that contribute to our ability to differentiate "me" from "not me." We don't feel anything when we see air being touched, so we come to feel air is "not me."

84 Some people, with the condition called anorexia nervosa, have distorted body maps. They may be very thin but when they view themselves in a mirror they see themselves, or parts of themselves, as being too fat. They then continue to eat sparingly and get even thinner, sometimes to the point of death.

85 In the late 1970s, when I was teaching in England, a fellow teacher arrived enthusiastically proclaiming the message of a group that said "you have no head." He couldn't talk coherently about the message, but I always thought it was connected to this topic.

86　There is a website that deals with material similar to that of this book. http://cns-alumni.bu.edu/~slehar/Lehar.html and my website www.museumofconsciousness.com, which is a prototype for a proposed actual museum.

87　Again check out the Lehar site mentioned in the above endnote.

88　Metzinger 2004 p. 548.

89　The term "hard problem" is attributed to David Chalmers.

90　John Searle is one of them.

91　Stuart Hameroff of the University of Arizona, and Roger Penrose.

92　See Jared Diamond's *Guns, Germs, and Steel* for a complete review of the spread of humans over the Earth.

93　When I was a student of physics, circa 1960, my father, having left the coal mines and begun working for the electric company, asked me to arbitrate a bet his fellow workers had made for $20. Does the Sun go around the Earth or vice versa?

94　While in graduate school, I brought home a telescope to show my parents.

The moon was full and we viewed its craters and maria, but my mother wanted to see the stars. I focused on a bright star and my mother peered through the telescope and then looked up— perplexed. "What's wrong, Mom?" After a while she said, "I don't see the points of the star." Even today, not everyone has absorbed the findings of the Renaissance.

95 Actually galaxies reside in clusters and it is the distance between clusters that is increasing.

96 Recently, a young man I knew from birth asked me to help him take his own life. Despite having caring people around him, he believed death to be a door to another life. At 25 he drowned himself. His belief could not be shaken.

97 See Daniel Dennett's *Breaking the Spell...Religion as a Natural Phenomenon* for an ambitious attempt to find out why people believe what they do, sometimes at great expense to themselves.

98 Get on the Internet and do a search on "world views." There are thousands

of ways people have of making sense of life. My attempt to classify them simply is embarrassingly feeble.

99 Damasio on page 110 of *The Feeling of What Happens* tells of a patient who, to remove a massive tumor, underwent an operation to remove his entire left hemisphere. Afterwards he retained his emotions, was awake and attentive, and behaved appropriately to his situation. The intactness of his core consciousness was not questioned.

100 See page 156 of his book *The Mystery of Consciousness*.

101 See Seth Lloyd's *Programming the Universe* for a description of quantum computing and how our universe may be performing such computations.

CPSIA information can be obtained
at www.ICGtesting.com
Printed in the USA
LVHW021225011222
734350LV00001B/111

9 781439 251447